Donald W. Dolson
2016

(416) 366-1414
donwdolson@yahoo.ca

Other Self-Published Books by the Author

Fact, Fancy and Philosophy (1970)
Heart Talk (1972)
Satire, Sentiment and Humour (1974)

Smaller Pamphlets
Let There Be Love
Feelings
In the Shadow of His Cross,

Plus:
GOD'S Creation—My Inspiration: 100 Poems
Copyright 2007 by Donald W. Dolson.
Watermark Press.

The Way I See My God. (story and poetry)
Copyright 2010 by Donald Dolson.
Guardian Books, Belleville, Ontario.

It Could Help a Young Man to Know (Social revelations plus
a selection of poems)
Copyright 2012 Donald Dolson.
Guardian Books, Belleville, Ontario.

THE GREATEST LOVE EVER SHOWN

IN THE FATHER'S HAND: GOD'S CREATION! OUR WORLD

DONALD DOLSON

WESTBOW° PRESS

A DIVISION OF THOMAS NELSON & ZONDERVAN

Back cover illustration by Donna Dolson

WestBow Press books may be ordered through
booksellers or by contacting:

WestBow Press
A Division of Thomas Nelson & Zondervan
1663 Liberty Drive
Bloomington, IN 47403
www.westbowpress.com
1 (866) 928-1240

Because of the dynamic nature of the Internet, any web addresses or
links contained in this book may have changed since publication and
may no longer be valid. The views expressed in this work are solely those
of the author and do not necessarily reflect the views of the publisher,
and the publisher hereby disclaims any responsibility for them.

Any people depicted in stock imagery provided by Thinkstock are
models, and such images are being used for illustrative purposes only.
Certain stock imagery © Thinkstock.

ISBN: 978-1-4908-6351-1 (sc)
ISBN: 978-1-4908-6352-8 (hc)
ISBN: 978-1-4908-6362-7 (e)

Library of Congress Control Number: 2014922164

Printed in the United States of America.

WestBow Press rev. date: 12/12/2014

Contents

CHRISTMASTIME - 118

This book is dedicated to furthering the Gospel, the melding of religious belief to scientific revelations by the original PHD in every kind of human activity by the Perfect heavenly Deity that we acknowledge as our God. I am eternally indebted to Him for my physical and spiritual life; He is an ever present help. Were it not for the Jews, there would be no Christians. Jesus was the most famous Jew who ever lived.

I seem to have inherited a trait from my Grandfather, Reverend E.C. Hall, preachers often repeat portions of their sermons for emphasis, and I seem to have done the same, I hope my readers will forgive me when they know what happened.

To my parents, Jack and Emma Dolson, for their loving care as I grew up on the farm.

To my brothers and sisters and school teachers.

To my first wife, Mary, for her love and loyalty, and to our daughters, Donna (now an art teacher) and Gail (a Phys. Ed teacher), plus my grandchildren David and Caitlin.

To my second wife, Ruth, for her help, love and devotion.

To friends in Fairbank Baptist Church, which became Ennerdale Road Baptist Church Toronto.

To my friends in Toronto Single Parents for their help during a trying time.

To my employers, especially Sigmund Knaul (deceased), the general manager of Coinamatic and my boss for 25 years, for his kindness and generosity. He had survived the Holocaust.

His wife, Marie; daughter Felicia (now a PhD) and son Jonathan (now a Major and a helicopter test pilot). We have been friends for many years.

To Mrs. Gloria Jay (deceased) and her family: Hilda (nurse), Richard (hematologist) and Danny (professor of Physiology at Tufts University). My children played with her children over 40 years ago. Gloria became Mrs. Paul Lee and he is now a widower.

Also to Mr. Howard Ely and his staff. I appreciated their encouragement at the International Society of Poets, where I was a life member for 14 years. Their friendly help and concern made possible my first book of poems, *God's Creation—My Inspiration,* in 2007.

Preface

This book is a compilation of a lifetime of learning experiences from family, friends, coworkers, church members, pastors, theologians and the Bible, plus professors in electronics, lecturers, and a series of publications and personal experiments over many years.

I had my first "horseshoe" magnet at about 8 years old and have been intrigued ever since. I had a Crystal set in my teens, read magazines and parts of electronic courses as well as official teaching manuals in home study courses, intermittently over the years, I was always short of money. It has taken me a lifetime to realize even a small part of the depth to which God will go to save each one of us from the grief to which temptations can lead us if we refuse to follow His directions for healthy, happy living. To know that He is an ever-present help in our times of trouble, and that He is always ready to forgive and forget our failures when we sincerely admit our mistakes, is very comforting. If we ask Him, He will help us to relinquish our will so that we can obey His. To know that without Him we can't do anything noble or God honouring is a very humbling experience but is entirely necessary for our well-being.

In the nearly 10 years I spent in Toronto Single Parents, I learned a lot from people in our discussion groups and in private conversations on my home phone, as well as from my coworkers in different jobs. I have learned that appreciation is the milk of human kindness that nourishes our innermost being. I have learned that praising God is our way of telling Him how glad we are for all He has said and done by sending us His son and maintaining our world.

We know that music, art and sculpture are visible ways of giving God glory, but how many realize that the menial tasks of caring for others are just as important? "Even as you have done it to the least of these, you have done it unto Me" says our Lord. He loves each of us.

This book is dedicated to show how God fashioned everything from His nought, and that regardless of our occupation there is only one source. Whether you choose to be a theologian or a scientist, you are part of one unit.

It is also tries to fill the hungry hearts of not only my friends and acquaintances whom I met and had the privilege of sharing our ups and downs (especially the downs), but of each person who might benefit from learning how other people have succeeded in rebalancing their lives. It was a deeply moving experience that no formal school of learning can duplicate. Anyone who has lost a significant other knows something of the anguish that comes from shattered hopes and dreams, but death is the deepest of them all. There is no way to say, "I'm sorry, I didn't understand, please forgive me. I didn't realize what you needed, or I could have made some changes if I'd known." That opportunity is gone forever; it's like an amputation of a part of you and your life, with no chance of turning back. It's lost, and an empty space remains that only God can fill. This realization alone can give you a giant step forward in your new life.

The fact that we all shared our heartbreaks; however they were caused, gave us a feeling of family and helped us to heal the best we could. Professional counsellors were helpful to a degree, but they were unable to be "family"; we couldn't phone them in the night when we often felt the loneliest, and unless they had known our kind of loss, empathy simply couldn't be there. Even if they had known it, they are constrained by their profession from being completely open, (I learned this personally) and without that ability their advice would seem inadequate for our situations. We lacked love, and it is my hope that having some more information from this book will help.

I have started at childhood to show that no matter how difficult your childhood was, you are the controller of how you think—but you have to ask God to help you relinquish your will so that He can help you to make the necessary changes to put you on the road of life if you've found yourself in a ditch somewhere. It was told nicely by Catherine Marshall, (wife of Peter Marshall one time Chaplain to a U.S. President.) in her book *Beyond Ourselves* where she admitted that she had to say a prayer of relinquishment to give God the opportunity to help her. Even though she had prayed "Thy will be done," she found she hadn't let go of her own will. Only you can do that.

I found that our road of life is similar to a country road full of ups and downs and with ditches on each side. Every so far along, there are some that look enticing because they are downgrade and easy to follow, but as you might expect, they lead into some kind of swamp, and you don't have a reverse gear—time can only go forward. As if that's not bad enough, even if you've avoided the swamp, as you go along you eventually come to a fork in the road.

One fork leads to married life, and the other leads to singleness initially. If you take the married road, in order to go on successfully you have to make big changes in your goals to accommodate someone with very different goals and abilities. It requires the ability of forgiving someone else and learning how to forgive yourself without rancour; this is where you can feel in control if you've learned how to let God into your life. You no longer feel like you're losing something when you accommodate the needs of someone else; it can actually feel like an accomplishment because you're helping something worthwhile and beneficial to happen to both of you.

After spending time in Toronto Single Parents, I got involved on the executive for our group, and helped as social action chairman, bulletin editor, and discussion group assistant. I got speakers, and I phoned members to let them know when and where our meetings would be held.

I often got calls at night without even knowing the name of the caller, because there was no call display back in the 1970s. I didn't mind because when talking about intimate problems incognito, at a distance is beneficial to both. The satisfaction I felt in being able to share seemed to negate the loss of sleep. Most of the callers were from women, but a social worker I had met at a sensitivity session of our club occasionally sent me a man she felt needed another male to talk to.

A young man phoned me one night. He was at home minding their two young children, and he was sick at heart with a feeling of a lump in his stomach while his wife was out with her girlfriends, possibly at a bar. I suggested she was trying to ease her frustration and hadn't known another way from her background. I don't know what all we talked about, but suddenly he said, "It's gone!"

I said, "What's gone?"

He remarked, "The lump in my stomach." I understood and hoped that he had found a way to empathize with his wife. I didn't hear from him again.

At about 2:00 AM one morning I got a call from a woman sobbing so much that at first I couldn't understand what she was trying to say. It turned out that she was sobbing "He never loved me" over and over again, and I learned she had just heard that her husband had committed suicide while she was living with another man. We talked until almost daylight, and I suggested that he must have loved her in his own way very much, if life wasn't worth living without her. It was obvious to me that he didn't know how to show his love in a way that she could understand. I pointed out he was self-sacrificing, because he didn't harm her or her new friend. When she calmed down, she told me that she wondered why he married her if he didn't really love her, and she had been labouring under the impression that she didn't have a real marriage. She phoned me a couple of days later to thank me for talking to her; she seemed composed and relieved that her marriage had been for real after all, in spite of sadness from misunderstanding.

Women's lib, unisex, a lack of honest disclosure of basic selves in even the counselling profession—these kinds of misunderstandings are all too common. Counsellors (both men and women) tend to be most concerned for the woman's side, condemning men for getting violent without pointing out that the differences between the way men and women comprehend words is at the root of much frustration and loss of patience. Dr. John Gray, in his book *Men Are from Mars, Women Are from Venus,* does a lot to dispel some of the mysteries surrounding human relationships. He tells women not to pursue a guy into his "cave." When a man has reached the end of his ability to fathom what his woman is trying to convey, he tends to try to walk away; he's had it for now. He doesn't want to hurt anybody, but he feels totally inadequate. Too often she pursues, to both their sorrows.

She is better with words; she has two segments in her brain for speech to his one. He is better at physical action; if she pursues, he may be pushed over his depth and resort to what he's better at—to his own chagrin, and her sorrow. A group of Plastic surgeons in the United States will repair damaged faces, but not until the women have had a course in human relations. Like the woman who continues to marry alcoholics, she is apt to have it happen again if she doesn't learn to control her tongue, she might get battered again. When you as a man know the source, you can avoid having this happen to you, and everybody concerned will be happier. Some men come from rough surroundings and simply perpetuate parental attitudes, but you can break the chain by using your intellect, realizing that what you allow yourself to think will eventually come out in what you feel you want to do; if you learn to understand and know how to forgive, your life cycle will come into happier times again, and those old flare-ups will seem inconsequential.

But it takes time, to work on thoughts and fantasies. The best compliment a man can earn is a happy wife. You have to be doing something right—and have her know it. I hope this book will shed some light in the dark corners. When men and women realize that God gave each one special but different talents so that together they are better able to face life's challenges through cooperating, then married life can feel like a blessing from God. God has shown the depth of His love by all the things He has created for us and by the sacrifices He made.

This book is an accumulation of things I have learned over a lifetime, both scientifically and sociologically. Too many good ideas have died with the inventor. I am told that I think outside the box. The box is made up of previous ideas, and from repetition it's considered by some to be the only truths.

From reading, experimenting and observing I find that quite a few so-called truths are inaccurate or inadequate from a common sense or simple logical point of view.

Early in life I had a curiosity for magnetism and things electrical and mechanical. I read books like *God and the Atom* by Victor J. Stengel, an atomic scientist, and his work does a masterful job of showing how intricate the particles are that make up our reality. I read an essay by astronomer Dr. John Lewinski, with his "super light" push gravity theory, and by astronomer Dr. Paul La Violette with his investigation into cosmic ray calamities when a huge blast of them strike our earth it can kill all forms of life in a wide area.(from Google)

Dr. Paul Corkum of the National Research Council, Ottawa, Canada, photographed an electron in 2010 and hoped to make a moving picture. (I met him in 2010 when he spoke at an R.C.I meeting in Toronto.) I especially admired Nikola Tesla, whose genius was not allowed to be fully utilized, as well as Albert Einstein and other highly gifted scientists. I realized that it took years to learn the foundation of mathematics even before higher math could be visualized; it is a language on its own, and the successes achieved are shown in the Mars Lander and in our everyday lives; "The latest achievement is by the European Space Agency, after about ten years chasing it, they landed their Rosetta Sattelite on a comet with little gravity" November 2014. (If gravity is the reciprocal of mass, the mass can be determined by its gravity.) In September 2014, in a science program put on by National Geographic on results of a satellite measuring the actions of our sun from The Goddard Space Center in the U.S.A., the announcer stated that the sun gets its power from "Push Gravity". I had assumed that gravity was a push, years ago, but I appreciate that the best I can do is a sketch from what I've learned from early deep thinkers like Galileo, Tesla, Fessenden, and even the Greeks, and from my personal experiences in my everyday world, viewing everything using simple logic and common sense from a grade school perspective.

My impetus comes from my personal acceptance of Christ as my saviour after having prayed for wisdom for years. In 1967 it happened at Fairbank Baptist church, when Eric Richardson of Open Air Campaigners from Australia held a weeklong rally there. He spoke like someone who had looked into Hell and didn't want anyone to go there. Without the insight Christ gave me, I wouldn't have the courage to write anything, but the outstanding deficit I encountered in my reading was a lack of any mention of God's Holy Spirit as the giver and maintainer of not only living things but in all inanimate objects. I got the impression that some people think when God put the world into being, with all that is mentioned in the Bible story of creation, He left us to carry on—but without His continued presence, everything He made would revert to empty space. Jews in the "Old Testament" were very conscious of God's presence. Christians state that when we accept Christ, we become part of His body, and with God's infinite wisdom we can expect Him to be conscious of His every part, us, and everyone else. If one of our parts is injured, our whole body knows it; if we harm someone else, we can be hurt as well because we're part of the same body (Christ), which ought to explain why it is essential for us to think and care for others because it eventually returns to help us in some way.

My eldest brother was in Home Defense on searchlight duty in Labrador during the Second World War. He got an inner ear infection that spread to his heart, and he was left with a permanently leaky heart. Books from ICS that he had acquired to study radio and electronics before army duty were a help to me in my teens. What happens to us early in life can affect our whole being permanently, which emphasizes the need to know God early in life if possible. Our mother told us about God, but I failed to understand even though she read some Bible to us almost nightly. I had seen our dad butcher a pig, and when Mother read us the stories in the Old Testament of the people dying in battle, I would get sick to my stomach. It gave me a fear of the Bible, though I knew God was good, I didn't feel loved until many years later, when I was born again. I had felt fearful for years. I heard and read plenty of Bible, but didn't note chapter or verse.

In everyday life it is simply expected that in order to be fair, we need to thank others for helping us in any way, and with God having done the most, it seems to me that we have failed miserably in our lack of showing Him our appreciation in truly meaningful ways by much of our population. We are deeply indebted to Him. He made us and all we have and can see, and He gave us His "operating instructions" on how we can have the longest, happiest, healthiest, guilt-free lives possible in His Ten Commandments, as well as follow-up instructions through writings by His prophets. Stating that "The wages of sin are death" looked to me like a literal observation, because if our lives were to be spent doing the actions banned in the last eight commandments, our disobedience could lead to our own demise, which could be avoided. It's our choice.

I have heard many sermons from a series of ministers from several denominations, (United, Presbyterian, Baptist, Catholic, Brethren Anglican, and a Synagog, different faiths. I find that a great emphasis has been placed on our unworthiness, and giving the congregation guilt trips week after week has made some people callous in self-defence when so many feel worthless already. Therefore membership has dropped off from many churches, and fewer people seek membership because there is so much disagreement between the various institutions of religious teaching. How can a person feel secure if those supposedly in the know can't agree among themselves, even within one denomination? God's word is obviously not taken seriously enough to inspire leaders to get their acts together, which is why I'm trying to point out that our God does behave like an earthly father who wants the best for His children. I've met people who had been going to church who quit going because of some insensitive remark by a church official. God's love is all encompassing regardless of what version of faith in Him we choose to follow, and He knows who is too often leading us astray.

I have learned and know that feelings are very important, and we are repeatedly told to evaluate our experiences on how we feel. However, it isn't usually emphasized that we need to evaluate how and what we feel by using our intellect to be sure our feelings aren't simply a momentary impulse that could endanger our future or that of someone else. Doing our duty can be distressful, but it's necessary, and the most long-lasting satisfaction comes from knowing we have done our best. While I was a member of Toronto Single Parents Associated, I observed that most people were doing the best they could with what they had in the situation they were in. This is where our club membership showed its ability to help: people learn more from observation than by being told. By sharing their various ways of coping, we helped some people to regain a sense of normalcy. I know I was, especially when I allowed Christ to come into my life. I considered our discussion group to be the best help for people really trying to improve their situations: we had about 300 members in our Toronto group, as well as connections to clubs in Leaside, Toronto, North Toronto, Scarborough and Mississauga. We arranged our dance dates so that there was some place to go almost every week. It helped to ease our sense of loss and loneliness. A few remarried, and I did so about ten years later.

We couldn't get many people to come out to our discussion groups if it was held in a church; the environment appeared to remind them of failings, even though we had a particularly good helper, Reverend Harold Burgess (now deceased), an AA, marriage, and interfaith counsellor in the 1960s and 1970s.

We held many discussions in private homes. There were other helpers, psychiatrists and social workers, as well as our primary speakers at our monthly educational and business meetings, but the ones with personal experience helped us the most by sharing their experiences.

Dr. Benjamin Schlessinger, head of social work at the University of Toronto in the 1960s and 1970s, told us, "I've come to learn from you guys, you're the ones with the experience." He did help through his expertise, and we saw him periodically, but learning the deepest secrets on how to live takes time.

As with much of our society, God was not in evidence except for some in profanity, the prevailing thought being, "If there is a loving God, how come He allows so much sorrow and doesn't stop wars or accidents?" I knew the feeling well: my daughters (8 and 12 years old) were on their way to church in one direction while their mother went in another and was struck and killed by a car a block from home. It took a long time, but I finally concluded that although He does intercede sometimes, if it would take away someone's free will, He simply takes our spirits home to be with Him, a better place by far. "I will repay, Saith the Lord!" Faith is the answer, and it's awfully hard to achieve sometimes, but it can be done when given time.

My basic hope is to get people to realize that God does love each of us, and He gave us His laws and rules so that we could fully enjoy this world that He created for our benefit, though it is only beginning to be known that from the moment of our Earth's beginning, it took God billions of our years to make it livable for us. The incredible timing of the solar system proves that God is the beginning of every kind of science; He is the source for every art or piece of knowledge. If we were to love Him as our father, and we loved our neighbours as much as we do ourselves, we would feel happy in doing what He has told us to do, and we would all be safe and secure in the knowledge that what we do now ensures our future here as well as in the hereafter. The miracle of creation begins with what is called nought, space, and proceeds in a seamless fashion from the tiniest element to the largest through His spiritual inspiration.

Those who stand in awe at the immensity and intricacy of even a grain of sand are privileged to show God a deep reverence, respect and love in the finest form of which humans are capable.

This book contains many bits of previous writings, but things that have happened since give a more complete picture of what it took me a lifetime to learn.

Chapter 1

The Greatest Love Ever Shown!

I call it the greatest love ever shown because it is—the evidence is all around us. We are told we were made from dust, and the ingredients were there, but it required the addition of a life spirit from God, the cooperation of bacteria, mould, fungus, and even viruses to work together harmoniously to create and repair all our various parts. Special cells are required to build hair, flesh, bone, nerves and brain cells, and that is not all.

Putting up with our rejection, misunderstanding and rebelliousness, required God to have infinite patience, love, forgiveness, mercy and pity; how else could He keep on waiting for our acceptance and gratitude?

I believe that love is a doing word, a life of voluntary effort for the good of others. We prove it by what we do.

There is a Bible story of the vineyard owner who went out in the morning to get workers, and he offered them 3 pence a day. He got a certain number, and He went out again at noon and got some more, offering the same 3 pence. In the evening He went out again, offering the same if they would come. Some of those who came in the morning were resentful of those receiving the same pay, when they had

1

been working far longer. However, the vineyard keeper is God, and the vineyard is our world. Those who accept Him in their early lives and are obedient are free from guilt, shame and many heartaches. The ones who accept Him in midlife, after having suffered, have more gratitude. Those who accept Christ near the end of their worldly journey can have a feeling of immense relief and gratitude, having suffered so long from their being unable (or unwilling) to follow the path God made for them, which had their best interests at heart. This can come from the fear of the unknown taking away our ability to trust and have unquestioning Faith. Stepping out as it were into what may seem a difficult path to follow requires the simple, trusting attitude of a little child, and Christ has said that unless we can adopt that attitude, we can in no way go to heaven.

Faith by itself is quite simple and can be found in the tiniest seed.

Our bodies were meant to be temples, and our faith is shown by our deeds.

As a loving father figure, God gave us His directions in His Ten Commandments as an outline of prescribed actions to avoid problems. He wants us to be more like His son Jesus, but like a sculptor fashioning a beautiful statue, the inspired words in our Gospel can little by little shape our understanding so that following God's path comes naturally and so that diversions, while observable, are not very tempting. We not only feel loved, we feel the satisfaction of accomplishment, like someone winning a race (our human race of living), and we can have sympathy for those who have fallen behind, knowing that we could have very easily been like them. You are not alone. All of those who started out in their morning of life are with you, and so are the ones who came later; we all become brothers and sisters in Christ when we finally understand and yield to His authority. Our job is to be an example of how a God-honouring person behaves in his or her everyday life. We learn to be more cooperative and less competitive, in order to give the less able an opportunity to have the satisfaction of proving to themselves that they have a right to be here and be included. In the Old Testament, in the story of Ruth, we read how Jews purposely left some grain in their fields so that poor people could help themselves.

I've been privileged to see the unselfish caring that demonstrates love in both humans and animals. I remember a little black-and-white barn cat on my Father's farm; she had learned to stand and open her mouth when we squirted milk at her when milking the cows. She was quite adept and enjoyed the milk. One day we missed her, so after doing the chores I looked around the stable and found her in a cow's manger having kittens, I stroked her, and there she was, purring all the time they were emerging. She constantly caught mice and brought them home to her babies when they were old enough for solid food.

At the same farm, we had a collie cattle dog that had her own house out in the yard, and Mother would take a bowl of food out to her every day. Suddenly the bowls started to go missing, and so Mother hid herself from Nancy's view. After Nancy got her bowl of food, she waited for Mother to go back in the house, and then she would look around, pick up the bowl in her mouth and take it to a hollow in our front field, where a male dog was waiting to be fed. A dog on welfare from a selfless female—the story had a familiar ring to it.

We saw the same sort of unselfish giving in both our mother fnd Father, most notable in the "dirty" thirties. We had no money for dentistry—we barely had enough to eat—so if someone had a bad toothache, we used a farmer's remedy. By folding a piece of paper into a cone shape and putting it on a cold plate, we lit it at the top, and it would burn down to the plate, leaving a few ashes and some almost clear, yellowish oil of smoke. It is quite poisonous, but by taking a toothpick and picking up a drop of the oil and putting it on the tooth, voila! no more toothache.

Mother's teeth would go bad every time she had a baby, and because we couldn't afford to have them taken out for years, the oil was used when necessary. When she did have her lower teeth removed all at one time, she went a long time before the uppers were also removed, and she had to gum her food until we had enough money to get false teeth. She was good at using her old foot-peddled Seamstress sewing machine, and because she didn't want people looking at her toothless mouth when singing in church, she made a hat with a veil to cover her face (she had learned millinery). She made our homemade bread and taught me how to as well; I still know how over 75 years later. I also learned how to make biscuits, and I liked to use sour cream or buttermilk in them for flavour. Mother had everything but drama in music; she played and sang in her father's church (Reverend E. C. Hall). His first church was in Franklindale, Pennsylvania, and was Christian denomination similar to Baptist; three of Mother's sisters are buried there. Our family of five boys and three girls all inherited artistic gifts from both our mother and father, Dad played an autoharp and mouthorgan simultaneously before meeting Mother. Music touches hearts.

Dad also lived through dire hardship, walking up and down after the horses and ploughing the fields while his varicose veins looked like ropes under his skin. They burned and itched, and he put a salve on them, but I'd seen him going to the barn to do the chores with shaky legs. The cattle horses and pigs couldn't be ignored—that was part of farming. Fortunately, his teeth stayed well for a long time, and he used a special toothpick made by cutting the quill of a big feather on a slant. It was thin and flexible, and if it wore out, he simply cut it back some more. We used a mixture of salt and soda to clean our mouths.

Dad had been up north deer hunting when he had a heart attack alone in the bush, and he had an out-of-body experience where he saw so much beauty that he didn't care if he got back home. God helped him to come back to show others that there really is a godly reward, and we learned that he had said his prayers beside his bed each night without his children knowing it, even on the night he died about a year later from a stroke. There were so many cars behind his hearse that people thought somebody famous had passed away, and they were right: he had been known as an honest helper in God's vineyard of life. Years before, at our farm near Palgrave, there was a stretch of road that would become muddy in the springtime. Dad would have the horses ready and pull our car through it when we got home from shopping in town. One day when he had finished towing our car through, a neighbour came along, and Dad offered to do the same for him. Dad said, "I guess you're Gates from up the road."

The man said, "I'm Mr. Gates to you!" Mr. Gates took a run at the muddy area with his car and sank down to the running boards, Dad walked into the muddy area, hooked onto his car, and pulled him out with his horses. He had hoped to hook on when on dry ground, but he just smiled and said nothing as Mr. Gates drove off in a huff. Dad hadn't meant to be disrespectful, and he didn't let it stop him from being neighbourly.

Cows can act like people, too. We had one young cow who disowned her calf; she would kick it away every time it tried to nurse. At the same time a big old red cow in another part of the stable would start bawling in sympathy for the calf when she heard its voice complaining—she wanted to mother it. We had to raise the calf ourselves with milk from the other cows; it would suck our fingers when we put its head into a pail of milk, and it soon learned how to drink from a pail.

On our farm we also raised ducks, and a little dark brown wild duck mated with our big white Peking drake. It was a comical looking pair: he was at least three times as large as she was. It takes three weeks to hatch hen's eggs, and four weeks for ducks. We put clucking hens (those in the mood to brood) on duck eggs sometimes. One year, a hen who had sat for three weeks thought she'd done enough, and so left her nest. If allowed to get too cold, the baby ducks still in the eggs would die. It happened that the little wild duck had just brought out her brood, and so we took them away from her at night and put the partly hatched eggs in her nest. She sat for another week and brought that batch out, too. The other ducks were much heavier, and so they crowded her out of the food when it was put out. She was so thin that she felt like a bunch of feathers and bone, but obviously she had a big heart. The "tame" ducks would not eat out of our hands, but the wild one would come up and take it from a can in our hands while protesting loudly. She took her final brood down to the creek, which ran through the front field of our farm, and in the fall her ducklings were better than the ones we'd raised.

> A little brown duck and a big white drake:
> see what a happy pair they make.
> She'll fly off down to the creek,
> but she'll be back within the week.

One of the wild duck's daughters, half again as big as she was, would fly down to the creek with her. She looked very pretty, with light brown and yellow markings—an adaptation between the white of her father and the dark brown colours of her mother.

We had picked the stones, fixed the fences and cleaned up some fields of twitch grass by smothering it with buckwheat (it has triangular leaf and keeps the grass from having sunlight). The owner now wanted his farm back. We moved away but came back a few days later to check things, and it was as if the spirit of the farm had died—no whir of wings, no quacking, just empty silence.

The greatest love ever shown is that of our God, who made our world and everything in it, above and below. He loves us so much that He calls us not only His friends but brothers and sisters in Christ, and He treats us as His children. God is both permissive and strict. He gave us a will so free that we can choose to not only ignore His directions on how we are to live to have the greatest joy, health and satisfaction, but we can even claim He doesn't exist. In spite of this abuse of His goodness to us, He makes it possible for us to change our minds and come back to Him, when we admit our mistakes and ask forgiveness through the shed blood of our saviour Jesus Christ; with our past forgiven, we can be spiritually born again. This has happened to people like John Newton, who once was the captain of a slave ship: he became a man of the cloth and not only served Christ, but he wrote the hymn "Amazing Grace" from his personal experience.

Over the centuries God has inspired many people in diverse ways to glorify Him in the prophetic portions of our Bible, in songs and in literature, in inventions, in service to others and in acts of unselfish bravery. No matter how horrible our acts may be, God can bring something good out of them through a change of heart in those involved, or in teaching those around us. As with any sketch, it is a basic outline where a foundation is erected and needs many smaller acts similar to sculpting. If we read our Judeo-Christian Bible carefully, we may find that in spite of our many imperfections, an image of the kind of people God wants us to be will emerge, and that image will have a Christ likeness to it. Jesus showed us how to obey His father's Ten Commandments, and He became the payment to fulfill God's edict of disobedience (sin) requiring the death of those not following His directions by showing contempt for the One who gave us life, liberty and the ability to be truly happy.

Native Canadians showed greater love for God than many of those who usurped their land; through their respect of everything surrounding them, they lived off the land without disturbing the rivers lakes and forests. Their view of God and creation is primitive according to our standards, but they show greater reverence even today—and yet we claim to love God but treat them as second class. If the money given them as welfare were instead considered to be royalties for our use of their land, they would feel much better.

According to my King James Bible, creation starts in Genesis. The authorship is attributed to Moses, who makes no attempt to give any scientific sequence but simply states the obvious. Even Moses could not have delved into the incredibly intricate workings of creation, and it wouldn't have been helpful even if he knew, because no human being can fathom the mind of one of such immense ability as our God. In the ensuing centuries, similar to the revelations given Moses, a person here and a person there has had portions of God's knowledge given to him or her, for which we should be grateful. If taken seriously, these portions indicate how complex even tiny things are and emphasize our need to show God gratitude.

Today's scientists have estimated that it takes trillions of what we call electrons to make even one grain of sand. Even the sand had to have a designer. These electrons appear to be formed from even smaller particles, called bosuns by Peter Higgs about 60 years ago. A Super Collider in Switzerland that scientists built to test out theories about particles finally concluded that the material God used is what we call space. God called it nought, and scientists now call them

God particles. They were His raw material. I think of space as the amniotic fluid of the universe, because everything is formed in it and of it. I don't know whether anyone has calculated how many God particles are in each electron, but they are obviously infinitely tiny. Their possible existence was seen years ago when an electron in a cyclotron nearing the speed of light appeared to disintegrate; it was said to "bloom," suggesting the electron had been made of those even smaller particles. With electrons being the essential part of atomic formation, it looked to me to be the beginning of a seamless sequence in the formation of matter, with one electron circling one atom, making hydrogen gas and with the addition of each electron revolving around an atom creating another material, each with bits of lesser parts. The original count was 100 combinations, and more were added with scientific creations (Einsteinium, for one).

These findings many centuries later would not have helped Moses explain creation to those early generations of people. His inspired vision was difficult enough. In trying to make a sketch of the happenings by using the work of many deep thinkers over the previous thousands of years, many of the people reading my writing today are unable to even imagine, much less accept, my own theory as being accurate, even though the theory came to me from my praying for wisdom and a lifetime of gathering bits and pieces after studying many texts and doing simple experiments on my own, hampered by the lack of finance and my own timidity. I found it difficult to realize how vulnerable we are, how vast and powerful nature around us is and how tiny we are in the total vastness of our universe.

Even though mathematics is essential in a majority of measurements, with God being a powerful Holy Spirit, we are told that "Things of the Spirit must be spiritually discerned" (1 Cor.2:14).

We can't weigh a spirit, and we can't measure the depth of feeling of love, loyalty, exuberance, the brightness of an idea or the warmth of an embrace. Many things have to be seen and felt through the faith of each individual in varying degrees, with ups and downs over time.

Each human being is a spirit clothed in flesh, to see and feel the many wonders of what God created for us. He gave us His directions on how to live a long, happy, healthy, guilt-free life if we will follow Him. Just before the Asian tsunami, I wrote this poem, which has seemed prophetic of happenings since.

God's Love

God loved the world so much, He sent His son
to save the souls of everyone
who would repent and follow in His way
along their pathways, every day.
God planned it all from up above,
but what are we doing to His love?
We see greed infect with every touch;
so many people want too much,
and God can hear the silent screams
of all lost children's hopes and dreams.
Wars and violence everywhere,
when those who have refuse to share.

It seems as though all nature mourns
with raging floods and violent storms;
fires light up the night time skies;
the air is filled with children's cries.
But through it all God's love remains
to cheer our hearts and ease our pain,
for He has promised us His peace within,
if we will place our trust in Him.

In today's world, the evidence of abuse of nature is all around us in the decimation of the honey bees, which are much-needed in the role of pollination for crops of fruit. The pesticides used to ensure close to perfection in fruit appearance are the obvious culprits, but financial profits for the here and now are being put ahead of long-term human survival. Other ways of pollination are being experimented with, but man-made alternatives cost money and increase our financial burden, creating an unnecessary dependency. Most insects have a special function to fulfill. Although many of the insects may be very annoying, they still are needed as food for many birds and even fish. They have become so scarce in some places that we don't hear bird songs any more. Fewer frogs are seen as well (Rachel Carson, *Silent Spring*).

Like a tourist going through a strange, awesome country, all I can do is a sketch, touching on what I have been privileged to discern, just as so many other people have done over the centuries. These sketches started even long before the Greeks: the various objects like Tutankhamen's gold mask, an example; that kind of expertise didn't come from an ape man. The "Hallelujah" chorus wasn't composed by formal education. Spurts of godly inspiration have punctuated every part of our world, and those who have these spells of inspiration come up from all segments of humanity, but they are not always recognized as such. A criminal can get the Victoria Cross for unselfishly giving his life even though previously condemned for murder like St. Paul's persecution of Christians, before his conversion on the road to Damascus. They say that beauty is in the eyes of the beholder and that beauty can be seen, heard or felt when we're touched by God. Great scientists have been privileged to do an autopsy on the physical portions of our world—the atom, the genes, the chromosomes, chemistry, things that can be seen, touched, smelt, or felt-- can use math to explain them.

Spiritual Eyes

No matter the shape or colour of our shell,
Inside; there dwells a human soul.
We do not always know and so cannot tell,
what we need to make us whole.
Some of us spend our whole lives dreaming,
failing to ever realize,
That to find the deepest of life's meaning,
we must look through spiritual eyes.
Always and forever some are yearning
to find a Haven for their soul.
Without God's grace there's no discerning
that heaven is our cherished goal.
Just as a worm turns to a butterfly

and wends its way to realms unknown,
in earth, at last, our human body lies
while our spirit seeks its heavenly home.
If our spirit is not encouraged to develop,
it can never take its flight,
but in the earth will ever be enveloped;
through all of the eternal night.
Are you learning humility, thankfulness and sharing
with the people you live and work with all around?
So your soul will be warm and fully ripe from caring
before your body is relinquished to the ground?
When we know it is God's love that we are seeking,
it seldom is a real surprise
that all the hungering souls within His keeping
peer out through ever hopeful eyes.

Math is in another realm; it is necessary but is not the only means of explanation. If we want to know about spiritual things, we have to go back to the original creator. People have been permitted to delve into many things, and we have marvellous computers, but man is now trying to develop a "quanta computer" said to utilize the ability to be here and there at the same time. This is entering the spiritual realm, where God is both here and there simultaneously. We are all parts of His body, and He can obviously feel everything touching His body even better than we can. With each of us within His body, He knows all of our hurts, hopes and joys. The evidence that there is another way of communicating that doesn't require using electrons has been shown many times, but it has been relegated to the realm of fantasy because it can't be touched or seen in order to be analyzed. An example was shown recently in a story in *Reader's Digest* with a pair of twin boys: one boy felt the pain from a growth developing in his twin brother's head even though they were many miles apart. The one with the tumour wasn't aware, but his twin was having bad headaches.

Although clairvoyance is frowned on in our Bible, it also says that by their fruits they are known; a bad tree cannot produce good fruit, and a good tree produces good fruit. If the result glorifies God, then it has to have some good in it. Some gifted people could be modern prophets. The valid prophesies came from spiritual inspiration; they weren't heard or read from human sources. Cases of knowledge achieved by using tea leaves have proven helpful sometimes, though it's condemned in scripture. Attributing a moment of godly revelation to an inanimate object is offensive to God, who deserves the credit. In England years ago, a little old lady who lived alone went missing; no trace of her could be found by police or neighbours. Finally, in desperation they went to a tea cup reader who seemed to have uncanny knowledge, and after looking into the leaves (her way of visualization), she said she saw this lady under a stone wall, but her face wasn't damaged. The police scoured her area and found where a wall had fallen down. Just as the tea reader had said, her face wasn't damaged. Who but God knew what had happened? This was in an article about strange happenings.

Marvellous things of God are spoken. This is very true, and the portion in the Anglican Book of Common Prayer where we say, "I am not worthy to even eat the crumbs that fall from His table." In other words, in God's sight I can be no more important than a worm on my own (my definition), but He tells us He considers us precious. He formed us in His image, and He wants us to know the joy of dwelling with Him, but we have to get to know Him and follow His instructions, found basically in His Ten Commandments. I see them as guard rails on our road of life; in order for me to have a long, happy, guilt-free life, I need to learn and follow them. We are saved by Grace and can't earn heaven by simply being good and dependable. We can't get paid unless we are doing our work as unto Him. We don't look any different to the world than the other guy, but he won't be there come payday (heaven) unless he has accepted God's authority and comes to Him in abject surrender. Like a human father, God wants the best for His children; He wantas to be able to feel proud of what He has accomplished, with the huge difference of His having given us a part of His spirit, clothed it with flesh and made us able to enjoy the other wonders that He created for our benefit.

We don't know what is in other people's hearts and minds—only God can know that—so I don't assume that if a person hasn't made an open commitment to Christ, the person is barred from heaven. God knows, and He will make a fair decision. People like Moses, King David and Saint Paul all made terrible mistakes but were used by God, so we have no right to assume what God will do.

God is not fickle and doesn't play games on us. What we see all around us is proof of His caring. The Bible says that there are no righteous, not one; this includes scribes and prophets who are imperfect humans, so if a portion of scripture is opposite from what His overall picture portrays; we can assume that a human made a slip.

Our Bible tells us when giving out a measure of goods, we are to heap it up to running over and be generous with our giving in order to honour God, but in another part we read of the "talents" given to a master's workmen to invest for profit. The one with three talents makes a nice increase, as does the one given two, getting praise from the boss. The third man, given one talent, observes that his boss "Reaps where he strawed not"—in other words, he gets money without working—so the servant gives him back the talent without interest and is cast into darkness with the "gnashing of teeth." He's damned for not being usurious with the money,(Parable of the three talents) even though we are told to be generous. It's apparently a real comfort to businessmen if we observe "Christians" flipping properties just like a man of the world, spending part of the future of our children and grandchildren.

With the increase in knowledge, people want God's love to be demystified. Sin is not a dirty cloud hanging over us even though it has our "Social Insurance Number" on it; it is the simple disobedience of failing to follow directions designed for our benefit by our loving father,

whether through ignorance or rebellion.

I've done more than my share of sinning over my earlier years, and I've asked forgiveness and been more deeply convinced than before of His sovereignty. We are told to "pray without ceasing," and it sounds impossible. (Muslims are told to pray five times a day, a literal physical display, but even that is not without ceasing.) I interpret it to mean a surrendered attitude, a consciousness of God's presence all the time. I have a long way to go, but when I know I've boobed, I think to myself, "Forgive me, God." I try to keep a short account.

Home

I often wandered by myself through
the fields that I called home.
It was after I went to the city that I really felt alone.
The trees had been friends of mine;
flowers would wave as I passed.
My broadloom was a carpet of sweetly scented grass.
A wet leaf might kiss my cheek as I
walked through a shady glen;
I felt at home and revelled in a world not made by men.
At night I could hear the sleepy peep of the birds,
and music of God's creation made a
song without any words.
I found in the city that the sights and sounds deceive;
and the smell of progress takes joy
from the air we breathe.
It was here that I found sadness; yet joy beyond compare,
for I know now that God loves us
and can find us anywhere.

As a loving father figure, God gave us His directions in His Ten Commandments as an outline of prescribed actions to avoid problems. He wants us to be more like Jesus,

Christmas Time (possible tune, Jingle bells)

(Chorus) Christmastime, Christmastime, oh what joy it brings
to know that we've been saved by grace by Jesus Christ, our king.

Happy throngs sing Christmas songs throughout the whole wide earth.
We congregate to celebrate the Baby Jesus's birth.

Before the world began, way back in time and space,
God envisioned man and planned the human race.
He also knew His son must leave His home in heaven
And give His life for everyone that we might be forgiven. (Chorus)

Angels brought the news to shepherds on the hills.
Wise men sought Him from afar, and wise men seek Him still.
He came to show us love, the best way to forgive.
His word sent from up above can teach us how to live. (Chorus)

When we accept God's son, His precious gift from heaven,
We then receive God's love and have our sins forgiven.
Following His way, we're very glad He came.
We celebrate His birth on Earth on the day on which He came. (Chorus)

Chapter 2

Creation as Seen by a Christian Layman

The story in Genesis starts a long time after God has decided to create a being in His image. It said that God, a powerful Holy Spirit, hovered over a ball of water. He has granted us an immense privilege in being able to analyze what He has been doing for countless centuries before the beginning of our story. We've been allowed to look into His workshop and see the origin of stars, the clouds of gas that eventually can become water as it did on our Earth. We can see the immense explosions in the birthing of new planets millions of years in the future, when portions have cooled and turned into round balls from the magnetic pull in all directions internally, putting them into their final shapes. But before that, there was a huge craggy rock that He formed first, still smoking hot from its violent beginning. We are permitted to know that because water has to be under air pressure to exist; it turns to gas under zero pressure. If the immensity of the privilege of knowing a portion of the steps God took to start the magnificent array of stars in the firmament were to be realized, we would volunteer to follow Him with eternal gratitude; if we did that, all the traps existing that He warns us of would not affect us if we followed His first two commandments, love the Lord with all our hearts and souls and our neighbours as ourselves. We would avoid most of the calamities now embracing our world. As with any huge construction job, steps have to be taken regardless of obstacles, and in the process human lives can be lost on this earth. But if we realize that each of us is one of His spirits, clothed in flesh and given the intelligence to appreciate the wonders in His creation, we will know He will take us back to His realm, which is far better. If we love Him enough to glean even a portion of His intentions, we would know that we can't lose if we trust Him with the lives He gives us. God purposely left a vacancy in us that only His spirit can fill, but He won't intrude—we have to give Him an invitation and promise to respect His directions to live.

When the Jews, long ago in times past, showed contempt for His directions, He punished them by having the Babylonians capture them and put them into bondage for 70 years. We have called into being millions of precious souls and then extinguished them through abortions, especially in Canada and the United States. More were lost in the past 10 years than were lost in the wars and the Holocaust in Europe. All of that was for our convenience, and we show contempt for His means of procreation through homosexuality.(I covered that in a copyrighted book titled "It could Help a Young Man to Know" by Donald Dolso, Essence publishing 2012". Muslims are related to the Jews through Hagar being impregnated by Abraham to create Ismael, as was Sarah, the mother of Isaac and Jacob, the Mother of the Jews. God promised He would make the

Jews into a great nation, and He did the same for Ishmael, but He did not design them to be adversaries. However, is it possible that the Muslims of today are scheduled to perform the role of the ancient Babylonians? We have incurred a huge debt to God for our disobedience of the rules He gave us, which were designed for our benefit. God is undoubtedly as disappointed as any concerned earthly father would be.

My interest in the physical formation of our earth started when I was young. I was initially into permanent magnetism, and I had my first horseshoe magnet from the magneto of a Model T Ford when I was about 8 years old (1934). In 1973 I was interviewed by Marq DeVilliers for an article in *The Toronto Star Weekly,* June 16, 1973. I thought we should be able to have an all magnetic motor, and it was treated as an elusive idea for perpetual motion but not considered as a real possibility. I learned later that Howard Johnson patented one that same year, printed in "Suppressed Inventions and Other Discoveries" by Jonathan Eisen, Patent #4,151,431, It worked, but parts prices made it uncompetitive, and the power it could generate was small though free. My interest started there but gradually encompassed the whole subject. I think it possible that with the proper additions, magnifying glass or glasses, mirrors, perhaps a quartz crystal or even something not yet discovered, we could produce a source of light without moving parts and producing no heat or noise. I base this idea on the fact that light is space pulsating in the optical segment of the electromagnetic spectrum, and that magnetism appears to be a flow of space. If we can cause a permanent magnetic field to oscillate in the optical range, we could have a source of light for people with little money in remote places after initial cost.

I had prayed to God for wisdom, but when the series of ideas started jelling about creation, I thought, *God, people will think I'm crazy. How could I be given knowledge beyond that of renowned scientists?* or was I privileged to be used by God as a conduit? I felt very unworthy. Were my ideas a revelation or simply imagination? Some people could look at it as science fiction.

Over several years the sequence of the parts used by God in our creation emerged. All the parts follow God's predetermined sequence. Even grass shows His love; our best scientists can't create a living thing. I had a series of experiences with things related to electronics, magnetism, pneumatics and mechanical experience, but it didn't start to get together until after my born-again experience in Fairbank Baptist Church in Toronto in 1967, about two years after my first wife, Mary, died from being struck by a car in 1965, leaving me with our 8- and 12-year-old daughters. I went into depression and was given medication to help me cope, but food tasted like sawdust, I wore a back brace, and I had trouble hearing, I tried to keep going for the sake of my kids. Eric Richards of Open Air Campaigners from Australia had held revival meetings for a week, and after several nights I felt like going forward to accept Christ after his sermons. The only passage of scripture I could remember was John 3:16, but it was sufficient. I thought I must have fallen in love with the soloist, and I suddenly felt as if I'd lost a heavy load. I felt happy, and after going home I still felt it, so I thought, *This must be due to the Holy Spirit,* because nothing else had happened. I was still on my own, but in the following days I found I could write my thoughts in poetic form almost as easily as breathing. I also found that my usual response when dropping something and breaking things, of a tensing of my stomach muscles and temptation to say some kind of epithet, disappeared.

In my first pamphlet of poetry, titled "Fact Fancy and Philosophy" (1970), containing over 50 poems relating to single parenthood, I relate the story of my conversion. I had been living in the hope of His forgiveness and justice without any real feeling of comfort. I was conscious of all the times it might have been possible for me to have helped Mary more. During the service Eric told the story of an evangelist who was setting up his soap box near a woolen mill at lunch hour. A worker observed him and asked him if he was a Christian. He said that he was, and so the worker said, "Have you made any mistakes since you've become a Christian?"

The man realized it was a loaded question! If he said he hadn't, he could be accused of lying; if he said he had, he would be hard put to justify his faith. so he replied, "I'll answer your question with another. Have you always worked for this woolen mill?"

"No, I used to work for one down the street," he replied.

"Have you made any mistakes since you've come to work at this woolen mill?" the evangelist asked him. "Oh, yes. Everyone makes mistakes," claimed the worker.

"Did your new boss accuse you of working for the mill down the street?"

"No, he just said I'd jolly well better not do it again!"

"Well," said the evangelist, "that's the way it's been with me since I've become a Christian. I've made mistakes, but He hasn't accused me of working for the devil."

In its home-spun way the story made me realize that simply hoping God would see my good works and pat me on the back for being a good little boy wouldn't get me to heaven, and if a public acceptance of Christ was all I had to do to receive Him, it was a very small thing to ask. I went to the front as if I had to catch a boat before it sailed. My emptiness went away immediately, and I felt as if I'd fallen in love. I wondered if it could be the soloist or the music. It didn't seem possible, but when the people were gone and I was alone, I still felt warm and wonderful. I realized I was blessed with the presence of a living savior, and by relaxing in His care, I found peace of heart and mind. If I try to analyze or figure out His works, I lose some of my feelings of security; it seems that acceptance of God is the key to making the world and all its people and problems look nicer, and life more livable. It's one of life's infinite paradoxes: it requires the least energy, but it is the hardest for most people to do.

Even though I received more warmth and comfort than I dreamed possible, I still hungered for a human's love. In a separate story I relate how I met a lovely lady and was smitten; I called her my Dream Girl, but like most dreams she didn't become a reality.

After joining Toronto Single Parents Associated later, I found out how satan hooks anyone who takes a stand for Christ, preying on our weeknesses, but I stopped straying and asked for His forgiveness, and He is true to His Word, even though I lost the original elation. Creation begins from His word and progresses according to the messages given to His prophets. His power brought everything into being and is still in evidence. The Greeks called space the Aether recognizing it as an entity, and Galileo stated that the earth circled the sun, contrary to the eminent thinkers of that time; he was ostracised for his assumption and even put under house arrest. Since then we've accepted that the earth circles the sun in an orbit, spinning at the same time at nearly 1,000 MPH at the equator, giving us night and day. The planet travels at over 60,000 MPH in its orbit around the sun. Later scientists thought of space as a vacuum, nothing, nil, but we couldn't get power from sunlight if that was true.

Today it has been recognized that the sun's emanations are high–frequency, direct-current impulses travelling like the waves on a pond, as do the light from the sun and stars. New findings are emerging, clarifying old theories and bringing out new ones based on later information. Minute parts have been thoroughly investigated, leading to new products and helping us in many ways, but we have a long way to go. If we can imagine ourselves in a frictionless and incompressible liquid, an invisible medium, we might comprehend that gravity is actually a push coming from the emanations of stars keeping our surroundings in a constant state of agitation, with objects appearing to be attracted to each other by external actions due to the fact that each object is shielding the other from outside and pushes toward each other, until centrifugal force, possibly from the objects rotating, prevents a collision.

It was thought for years that what we call gravity (Sir Isaac Newton's idea) was some kind of attraction or suction, but we couldn't have a volcano if that was true. Volcanoes exhibit effects of high pressure and intense heat from inside the earth—perhaps a diesel effect from space pressure? Air pressure at sea level is 14.7 pounds per square inch, it's over 46,000 tons on an acre of land.

Some scientists have suggested that atomic reactions provide the heat to keep lava in the center of our earth liquid, but volcanoes don't spew out radioactive material. Some volcanic ash acts as a fertilizer.

There is evidence now that gravity is a push, possibly created by electrons being opaque to space, movement coming in all directions as high-frequency waves from the sun and stars feed their energy into our incompressible, frictionless surroundings. No matter the frequency, each wave contains a tiny portion of the energy from its originator. All good things come from above—a biblical statement. If star waves are part of the gravity picture, why don't things weigh differently at night than in the daytime? Perhaps the immense pressure exerted by the huge stars in the incompressible medium we call space collectively override the portion sent out by our sun.

The sun seems to provide our rotation by hitting on a slant due to the angle of our magnetic poles, by the "skin effect" as observed on bladeless turbines. You may wonder how things in space can turn so easily with all the waves from the countless stars striking us from all sides, but it may help by realizing that even at high frequency, each wave is a separate bit of energy. We see starlight, but they may be sending frequencies both higher and lower as well, coming at the same time. Each heavenly body will contribute to the many separate impulses in this frictionless, incompressible material we call space, which appears to be under infinite pressure in order to faithfully reproduce impulses up to and including that of light, between 430–790 trillion Hertz, (cycles) per second (Google, Wikipedia, the free Encyclopedia), with light being the most obvious. Light is only seen when it strikes some kind of object; this is observable in a movie theater, where the images from the projector show up when they strike the screen. This concept explains why the night sky isn't bright.

Everything we see, hear or feel is in relation to something else. Nature has a habit of using the same action on different levels. No matter the name given to the different emanations, they are all space.

On a hot day on our farm, I've seen tiny whirlwinds (dust devils) throw dust in the air for a few seconds, but when a bigger whirlwind went across our hay field, I saw it dismantle hay cocks and throw the hay high in the air, leaving us to rake it up again. Storm chasers in the United States found that tornados have very low pressure internally, from centrifugal force throwing air outwards, lowering its inner pressure and facilitating lightening strikes, because electrons can float freely in space. I've seen layers of clouds going in different directions and picking up electrons from each other, facilitating thunder storms. We see sheet lightning from cloud to cloud, as well as lightning bolts from cloud to ground. Some are single strikes, but others oscillate until charges are dissipated.

This fact has been utilized in the vacuum tubes used in radio and television. It creates a problem in hermetic compressors used in refrigeration and air-conditioning in that if there are too many cracks in the insulation on the wires in the motor when the unit has been pumped down to a near vacuum, electrons escaping into the lower air pressure can cause the motor to heat up and burn out. Air under atmospheric pressure keeps the electrons on our power wires and in our electrical units, making the use of electricity possible in a large number of ways.

Objects in space have to be well insulated in order to function properly. Tornados are concentrated vortexes of moving air and are extreme whirlwinds; hurricanes cover more territory and as a rule don't have as high speed at the center, but they can cause a huge amount of damage over a wide area.

What I've called the Dolson Theory came later, after years of praying for wisdom about Electricity, Magnetism and space—the GEMS of God's creation. It came to me gradually over a long period of time after 1967, when I had my born-again experience. I read, did minor experiments, studied and worked at radio and television as a hobby, hoping someday to be able to work at a job with less dirt and more satisfaction. I earned a TV serviceman's RETS certificate in 1957 in radio and television repair. In 1958 I passed a course at North Metro Emergency Measures Organization (Toronto), led by Mr. Paul Tuz, in basic rescue, St. John's Ambulance first aid, Technique of Instruction, and radiation monitoring (due to the atom bomb scare).

I learned that the radiation people were exposed to showed up on a dosimeter, which you wear on your wrist and which uses a negatively charged quartz fiber needle. It measures the amount of energy reradiating in the worker's blood, and it takes electrons from the needle causing it to move, indicating the level of radiation received. This implied to me that bosons (space particles) flying out of atoms, like sparks from a grinding wheel were dismantling electrons, turning them back into the space from which they came. Could this mean that if we were to put a terminal on a lead shield surrounding a fuel rod, and we electrically insulated the combination from the Earth, we could get direct current? The radiation removes electrons, and so that terminal would be positive and the earth's ground would be negative. It's an idea worth trying.

The centrifugal force on sped-up atoms seemed to be throwing off bosons. Large atoms spin longer, extending their time of radiation; they still get the impulses that kept them rotating before, and with space being almost frictionless, they take a long time to slow down and stop radiating. This is my opinion.

Later, I had a retraining program at Standard Engineering in air-conditioning, refrigeration, appliance repair and oil burner servicing around 1960. I had 600 satisfied customers for a season, and I had been working as a franchised agent of Toronto Fuels.

Starting in 1946, when I first came to Toronto, I earned a "P" license in auto body spray painting, and a "B" license in auto body repair. I had started repairing radios and small appliances in my teens from what I'd read in a variety of books and magazines—*Popular Mechanics, Mechanics Illustrated, Science and Mechanics* and others, including a partial course of home study at International Correspondence Schools. I developed Meniere's disease (a loss of balance condition) about then and had to stop taking that course, but I went to RETS studies in radio and television years later.

George Louis Le Sage had suggested a push gravity idea in 1748; he called his particles in space "ultra mundane corpuscles" and expected them to be pushed together in space by one shielding each other from space pressure. He knew eminent thinkers of that time. I envision a similar action, but I call them electrons. The space particles (Higgs-bosons) are what I call magnetons, because they are what flows to create our magnetic effect. When electrons flow, putting them into a circuit, they are what makes up the volume of the flow. A permanent magnet illustrates the effect going on around each atom, and this effect seems to be maintained by the stars and our moving through space. I experimented with permanent magnets and noticed how like poles repelled each other. I wondered if it was because we are in the equivalent of a closed circuit. When space flows in one way, there has to be centripetal action flowing equal and opposite to balance the effect.

Electrons moving through space produce a magnetic field. (I saw this illustrated by a teacher using an Amprobe while studying at Standard Engineering in Toronto.) I thought of it as a Newton moment (referred to elsewhere), and I thought that a magnetic effect appeared to be created by space flowing like a liquid rather than simply passing on each vibration. Some scientists refer to a large amount of space as dark matter, which is unidentified as to its role. It appears to me that space is the most complex material in all of what God has created; it faithfully retains the speed, intensity and shape of the waves coming simultaneously in all directions, and it's totally inert with no movement or power of its own. It is an infinitely complex entity.

On April 29, 2012, scientists at the Super Collider in Switzerland stated their finding of "the God particle," formerly called the Higgs-Boson because Peter Higgs had suggested it 60 years previously.

The most basic material, the dark matter, is what God made everything from—His nought. Scientists called it a vacuum of nothing, but we can't have a wave of nothing, and the sun's power couldn't reach us if it were.

I've gone ahead on my own, analyzing everything from simple logic and common sense. Impact drills vibrate vertically to assist penetration to drill holes in concrete. The waves coming from our sun and stars are composed of high-frequency, direct-current waves, possibly giving them the ability to penetrate our earth and everything on it or in it. I believe that when God called our universe into being by His power, He continued to use His power to maintain it. Without His sustenance, everything could revert to the void from which it came. The sun and stars appear to have used the space particles to create individual electrons in the suns.

Dr. Paul Corkum of the National Research Council in Ottawa, Canada, photographed an electron in 2010 using a laser flash of one Ato second 1/000,000,000,000,000,00 0,000,000[th] of a second. He hopes to get a moving picture of electrons in motion. Electrons, along with a number of other particles, assemble to make atoms. With every change in the number of electrons circling the core, a new element emerges with its own combination of abilities. When a group of atoms combine, they become a particle. A grain of sand contains trillions of electrons. How many electrons does it take to make a human being? What is a spirit? Aren't spirits responsible for allowing us to enjoy life? Do they give us our thinking power? God created people in His image to enjoy the wonders of His creation. Einstein suggested that space must be made up of millions of particles, and I believe him. He opened the door to a whole new era. Einstein also suggested that we can't travel faster than the speed of light; this seems obvious when years ago scientists sped up an electron to near the speed of light in a cyclotron and saw it bloom, seeming to turn into many particles. Aircraft builders in Malton, Ontario also discovered that the standard method of forming flares on tubes handling fluids for air-conditioning and other uses was unsatisfactory for military aircraft, because the flaring caused the tube flares to be brittle and break from vibration. They discovered that by putting the tubing in a special jig and passing an intense field of magnetism (measured in Joules), the tube could be flared by relocating the molecules without heat or pressure, which meant the flare was not subject to breaking from vibration. The mettle even expanded a bit because the atoms could arrange themselves at an optimum distance from each other. This system also made it possible to create new things. With magnetism appearing to be space in motion, it suggests that if we were to travel in a spacecraft at or near the speed of light, (186,300 miles per second) our craft could disintegrate. Even at a lower speed, if we met a space wave travelling in the opposite direction, it could add to the effect.

I was not surprised to hear of the cores of magnets melting when the Super Collider magnets were first energized. Intense magnetic flow had already proved its ability to separate atoms in the flaring of aircraft tubing.

I think that what I observed of the Amprobe measuring magnetic flux is similar to Dr. Newton's observation of gravity—another revelation pointing to other possibilities.

This suggested to me that any object forced to travel near the speed of light would disintegrate into its electronic and atomic particles in a huge flash of light (light being space, vibrating at the optical segment of the electromagnetic spectrum of space vibrations). It was recently stated that Einstein was wrong in that a neutrino experiment appeared to show that neutrinos travel faster than light, but that wouldn't make any difference. Neutrinos split atoms; they don't appear to be part of the building blocks in creation. Though they are an integral part of the atom, Einstein would still be right. We seem to have failed to realize that anything spinning will have gyroscopic and centripetal action (the flow of fluid to replace that which has been flung outward by centrifugal force), and that the combined effect of the countless spinning elements keep solid objects in place; we call it inertia. Star waves arrive as shafts of energy in a direct line, giving us our gravity by pushing on the electrons in all matter from all directions. When an object rotates, it can't be hit directly, and so much of its downward push effect assists in making it rotate. I read that aircraft carriers utilize this effect by using large gyros to steady their flight decks to help the take-off and landing of aircraft. Downward push of gravity waves being flung outward by centrifugal force are similar to the action in a gyroscopic compass.

The gyro compass is well-known, but how many people realize why and how it operates to show direction? God's works are intricate and infinite with many inscrutable, unfailing laws in each and all of His created objects; be they in physics, electronics, chemistry, atomic, the physical world or His spiritual world. All work together in a seamless, sequential order if we believe His word and follow His directions, which have existed since time began, but many are yet to be discovered. Spiritual things require spiritual discernment and faith in God's goodness in order to be disclosed, and though mathematics is a necessary tool, in many areas it can't measure the depth of our love, loyalty or convictions, or how bright an idea is, or how thoughts originate. Human conception and the origin of ideas or feelings are other domains that remain mysterious through our lack of faith, the substance of things unseen and a very important part of creation necessary to inspire our trust, joy and loyalty. Faith is a reason for living, for things to give our lives meaning and purpose.

If you have watched a ball floating on a body of water, you may have noticed that it requires a series of waves to bring it to the shore. The ball has inertia, and the water has a little friction. The spinning electrons and atoms in its makeup make gyroscopic action and inertia, and so many waves go under it before it reaches shore. An object in space where star waves can reach it from all sides retains its momentum because of space being almost frictionless. It's retarded by the viscosity of space; once put into motion with waves coming from all sides, the effect on the object's movement is zero. Space waves striking each other in space cancel out, but when striking the Earth they penetrate as one impulse after another presses on the surface. Their energy eventually ends up making heat in the Earth's core from the suppression of electrons inhibiting space movement, being opaque to space movement, which is why mass suppresses radiation, and radiation (like everything else we observe) is a certain way that space moves. Space can move electrons, and a laser light with greater intensity in that spectrum can be used to drill or cut by disintegrating electrons, which to me means we don't have slag showing after the cut; even with metal, the material appears to revert to the space it was composed of.

I go from the tiny to the gigantic. Our sun sends out huge clouds of electrons with a wide variation of vibrations in the electromagnetic spectrum. Even though each wave is tiny, it is not an alternating current because it travels in one direction, and so it is considered a direct current carrying the necessities of life over millions of miles in all directions. Stars thousands of times larger than our sun feed their radiation into this incompressible medium we call space, and because they come from all directions, they keep space vibrating at countless frequencies with harmonics and heterodyning occurring all around us.

Tesla had the idea that he could harness some of this power so that each home could be self-sufficient without the need for power wires crossing our communities. If we were to build on his idea and find how to convert gravity waves into electricity, many of our pollution problems would be solved. He knew how, but we failed to get it.

A radiometer shows how light can cause rotation, and I have wondered if sunlight shining obliquely on our Earth causes it to rotate (skin effect), and if the starlight arriving from all directions is responsible for keeping electrons and atoms spinning, simultaneously creating centrifugal force, gyroscopic and centripetal action, which might explain the maintenance of solid objects.

The fact that we can send and receive messages over millions of miles of space with a 10–20 watt transmitter on Mars indicates to me that we are under infinite pressure in an incompressible, frictionless medium.

Sir Frances Bacon insisted on proof before accepting a theory. I believe that many of my assumptions have already been proven by scientists in the past, which is evident by the observable actions I have shared. Common sense and simple logic help.

The output of stars in this incompressible entity we call space has a direct effect on all other heavenly bodies. God is in touch with all of His creations, from the tiniest to the indescribable gigantic. We simply do not have enough intellectual capacity to understand it all.

According to Dr. Paul LaViolette,(astronomer) cosmic rays can strike the Earth in shafts of energy with immense destructive power. A small shaft hitting an ocean could create a tsunami by putting pressure on the water and causing a tectonic plate to subduct from the added pressure. In the Asian tsunami, the water had appeared troubled. at the start(blow in a glass of water and see the effect). Animals headed for higher ground; a small increase in air pressure in their ears could indicate the need. As the plate rose, pulling the ocean up like a blanket, it caused water to recede from the shore when an adjacent plate went under it. Fish swimming against the flow ended up on the beach. He suggested that a huge cosmic ray burst from ten to twelve thousand years ago struck the earth and eliminated most of the life at that time.

Huge piles of bones can be found near Siberia, and Mastodon steaks were being eaten in New York City in the 1930s when I was a boy. The animals had been frozen so fast that green food was still in their mouths. If a blast like that hit our Earth on a slant, the surface could be momentarily retarded, and the core's momentum could cause tectonic plates to build mountain ranges while a gigantic flood engulfed everything. If the mountain chain directions were to be noted, the rotation of the Earth at that time would be revealed, and if the age of the ranges could be accurately evaluated, the time between each of these occurrences could be found. I feel that we are very vulnerable to the power of Nature (God). Deep channels in the ocean could explain where mountain bulk came from.

Our sun's light puts a measurable pressure on our Earth; with the Earth spinning, a progressive area becomes flooded with light, and I wondered if this is what causes our world to rotate, as I've already mentioned. If our Earth were to suddenly slow down because it was struck by a cosmic or gamma ray burst, there would be a huge flood from the momentum in oceans that could engulf much of the land. This may have happened before (at the time of Noah). It could have taken time for the world to regain its speed of rotation. This action could have caused civilization to start over, heralding another era. Geologic studies indicate this to be a possibility in our past. To my mind the pushing power that causes our Earth to rotate could be causing the tectonic plate movement, because our world is made up of so many pieces, with nothing solid to push on, and it's subject to the movement of many other heavenly bodies.

Everything appears to be dependent on the constant output of our sun and stars keeping space vibrating at a countless range of frequencies, with each segment in the electromagnetic spectrum performing another function. Heat is felt at the infrared region; above that is the visible light segment, 430 trillion vibrations or more per second depending on what color one is observing.

I suspect that our sun is causing our world to rotate by hitting us on a slant, and I hope to have some proof by floating a plastic ball covered internally with reduced iron in a glass bowl of water, using a magnet underneath it to hold the ball in place so that it can turn around when I shine a light slantwise on it.

The magnetic poles of our Earth hold us on an angle so as to maintain our attitude, which is the originator of our seasons and our day and night. When our world reversed its poles in the past, it is possible that it also caused our Arctic and Antarctic to appear on other parts of our earth, which has already happened in our distant past. This implies to me that a period of instability may have occurred before we regained a positive sequence, and that seems to depend on us having magnetic poles to keep our Earth aligned to give us dependable times for night and day. Ancient history has noted that the sun rose and set at opposite sides long ago as well. Someone has expressed the fear that our air could be compromised by pole reversal; ultraviolet radiation could cause drastic changes in some areas of vegetation with the loss of our magnetic field for a period of time. But can we be sufficiently concerned to avoid a nuclear holocaust? If you can conceive that it is star waves that hold our oxygen onto the Earth, we will still have breathable air; much of our oxygen is derived from our ocean's algae and other plant life, so we need to take more care of our oceans' waters by finding a way to reduce polluting it.

Stars emit huge quantities of electromagnetic vibrations over a wide range of frequencies on the electromagnetic spectrum, which we have not been able to harness up to now. Nikola Tesla was close, but he wasn't helped enough. The fact that we see the light of stars proves they reach our world with their emanations from every direction, reaching us billions of years after their creation. I see them as creating weight from electrons being opaque to space movement. Air is made of atoms and electrons. Move either space or electrons, and the other is moved. This is responsible for all electronic transmissions.

A much greater fear could be the cycle that Dr. Paul LaViolette observed of cosmic ray bursts, which appear to have struck our Earth at between 10 and 12 thousand year cycles. Between approximately AD 800–1200, Greenland was farmed until the weather got too cold to grow crops. We have made some difference in our weather by what we have done and still are doing, but the big picture indicates that something much greater still has the most say, and we need to consider our neighbours as friends and brothers and sisters in Christ in order to have sufficient peace and tranquility to enjoy the many blessings that are all around us on a daily basis. Cooperation rather than competition needs to be our watchword. When we each care for one another, everybody is safe; we need faith.

Before creating human beings in His likeness, God made a whole universe of suns, moons and stars. The sun warmed the earth and made possible vegetation for animals, us, and other creatures. God then made us, with adequate provisions for our needs and instructions on how to survive and enjoy what He had made, but by exercising the free will He gave us, we chose to go away from Him even though He sent us guard rails of instruction in the form of the Ten Commandments. At first, after warning people of the dangers of disobeying Him, (sinning), His edict declared that death was the penalty. He made provisions for having us forgiven by asking His forgiveness and paying a penalty through giving an animal or bird to be sacrificed for atonement.

We still wandered away, so to make doubly sure we understood, He projected a part of His Holy Spirit into the womb of a young virgin, and he had His son go through all the human sequences of growing up in a human body in the home of an ordinary carpenter with brothers and sisters to show to humanity that God knew all the feelings of His human beings and made allowances for their failings. God is delighted to see us choose to follow His instruction, but His instructions are to keep us out of trouble, not simply to gratify Him. Few people seem to realize how affectionately God regards all of His created beings. Disobedience of His laws are called sins, and they have our "Social Insurance Number" all right, but God prefers to save us.

His original edict was death for disobedience, which to me was an obvious result. Regarding disobedience for stealing, murdering and adultery, physical death could be a natural result through physical damage or contracted diseases. He warned us for our own good, because He knows from the beginning to the end, and He asks us to choose life.

Over the centuries people gradually learned to make tools and a host of objects while observing the heavens and coming to a variety of conclusions over thousands of our years. Little by little God permitted us to analyze parts of His creation and to do what I call an autopsy on it. We've come a long way toward discovering what our world is made of, and we have started to experiment with vital parts of God's creation, especially the atom and its parts, the main powerful element in everything. But God did not reveal what life is, or how a heartbeat is established in the sinus node of each heart. Neither can we determine the origin of thoughts or analyze them, or what we call our spirits. They are actually His, and we are permitted to use them. He hopes we will appreciate the privilege; I think of people as spirits with bodies to praise and glorify God for the privilege of enjoying the many beautiful things He has given us to use. God did not give us the knowledge we would need to fully understand everything; we don't have the mental capacity to do it, even at the start of creation, and we still don't have it. We are not expected to usurp the role of God—if we do, we are in danger of His wrath. Life and death are His to determine; each spirit of life given to a human egg is precious to Him.

We haven't been told how God created everything from His nought, but we've learned about electrons, atoms and associated parts, and we've tapped into their power. We haven't fully respected how powerful and dangerous it can be to our future existence. Neither are we aware of the immense power around us, or how over many centuries our Earth has been changed by being struck by other heavenly bodies. Geologic evidence, with the burial of coal, salt and potash thousands of feet underground, shows that our world has been stirred like a pail of mud in the far distant past. We've been told that the Colorado River created the Grand Canyon in the United States, but if that were so, there would have been a huge projection of earth into the ocean from the cubic miles of soil and stones from the area involved. When I saw it, it looked to me as if a heavenly body struck our earth so hard from the opposite side that our Earth cracked open, and the river simply followed the easiest route on top of that, the sides of the Grand Canyon are thousands of feet above sea level at its mouth, 4,800 on the west side, 7,000 feet on the south side, and 8,000 feet on the north side. Water doesn't run uphill. Adjacent to it is the remains of a petrified forest, showing that that area was at some time submerged in water. North of that area in Canada, we have the prairie provinces, which are about 500 feet above sea level (higher or lower depending on the area observed), and potash mines in Manitoba are deep underground; one is listed at 4,400 feet (Google Manitoba potash mines). One source of potash is the decayed remnants of Bracken fern, but mainly it is trees that have been subjected to a high temperature, like the making of coke, especially elm. This underground area was once on top thousands of years ago, if that is how it has been created. On top of the Grand Canyon, snail shells are there, and in the Canadian west at Drumheller Alberta and in the Rocky Mountains, our world has gone through vast changes and is still changing. We have to change, too, if we are going to have a successful future by being more respectful of God, of each other and of our environment.

Native people have been (and still are) more respectful of God's creations, even though we don't follow their perception of how it all started. They have shown the greatest love for their creator, God, by their respect for all of nature.

Native people have been treated badly, have been misunderstood and have had their land and mineral rights taken away—as well as their children. They are our hosts because they were never conquered and were not paid for much of what is now called Crown land in Canada, yet governments have given building rights to developers on land not clearly owned by our government because it wasn't bought, traded for or ceded by natives.

Much is made of the "welfare" paid to Natives. If it was to be considered royalties, as it would be if white men owned it, the natives could have a better sense of self-worth instead of feeling perpetually cheated, and they could be given proper respect. Without their participation in the War of 1812, we might not even have what we call our Canada.

When we acknowledge the worth of God's creations, we show respect for God and are blessed by Him. Some people ask, "If God made us and all we see, who made Him and all that space material He used to make everything out of, if in fact that is what happened?" If anyone could answer that, it wouldn't be a human being, but someone with the knowledge of God, and He knows we would not be able to understand even if we were told; we don't have that ability, and God knows it. He has been giving us little bits of knowledge over centuries of our time as we have become able to accept concepts unknown in the past. This ability has come in spurts. The Greeks were able to fathom things not accepted by later civilizations, which could have had us further ahead in our accumulation of bits and pieces that make up the world in which we live. If a person can accept the idea that electrons are made from tiny bits of space material, and that an electron is opaque to space movement, a lot of other pieces automatically fall into place. The connection between gravity, electricity and magnetism becomes logical, and the whole collection of activities from the individual portions of the electromagnetic spectrum can fall into place. No matter what we call a segment of the electromagnetic spectrum—AM, FM, short-wave, VHF, UHF, SDHF, infrared rays, light, and the whole gamut of higher frequencies—they are all parts of space in specific parts of the electromagnetic spectrum. Whatever we call them, the name denotes a certain activity, not a type of material.

I've been having difficulty finding anyone who can comprehend what I've been writing about, and so I will go back to the beginning of how waves react. If we drop a pebble in water and watch the circle of waves starting at the point of entry, and we watch as the waves go outward, diminishing as the energy is depleted, then we see that the waves go only outward—they don't reverse their motion. We are observing direct current impulses. This type of action is repeated many times in various portions of creation. The power from our sun arrives in the same way: the ripples of direct current energy spread out like the ripples on a pond, but they are a combination of very high-frequency, direct-current impulses.

With space surrounding everything and waves able to go in all directions at all times, it becomes harder to visualize the reactions out in space.

This suggests that light is space vibrating at trillions of impulses per second. The sun emits frequencies both higher and lower; heat comes from the infrared lower end of the light spectrum of frequencies. At a much higher level, above our light spectrum we reach ultraviolet, which can tan or burn us. Frequencies of impulses above that segment of the electromagnetic spectrum can neither be felt nor seen.

The repetition of similar actions is repeated many times by nature. When we hold up a steady hand, it is accomplished by a rapid sequence of nerve impulses synchronized by our brain to pull the proper individual strands of muscles necessary to produce the action desired by our minds. Warm-blooded creatures have high-speed muscle activity to produce heat; when we feel cold, speed slows down and the contractions become more violent. When we shiver, our body is trying to increase its warmth. This takes energy, and it explains why cold-blooded creatures require less food to exist and move about; they require heat from the sun to be able to live and procreate.

One hears of black holes out in space; to me, they are vortexes of space similar to the tiny ones we can see travelling downstream in a shallow brook. Though at the bottom of the stream, the rocks and undulations don't change, these tiny vortexes do. Space reacts like liquid of a very light viscosity, so much so that a ripple of light travels at 186,000,300 miles per second. The fact that we see stars means that their rays reach us, and their collective emanations keep all of space in a constant state of activity.

High-frequency beams travel in straight lines, and because each one carries a small portion of its original energy, they constantly strike our Earth from all sides. With the ability of electrons to move space, and of space to move electrons, these beams strike the gas molecules in our atmosphere pressing them against our Earth, creating our air pressure and what we call gravity, because the mass of the Earth keeps star beams from travelling through from the other side. It is possible (to me, at least) that this energy ends up creating the heat in the core of the Earth, and contrary to our present scientific thinking, the intense pressure may be what creates the molten iron in our core, which gives us the ability to have magnetic poles, which as I mentioned earlier are very important to our well being.

A question: how could we have volcanoes if gravity is a suction or attraction? It makes no logical sense, and this very delicately balanced moon sequence, as it travels around the Earth, prevents star waves from reaching a portion of our Earth on a sequential basis. This creates an area of lower space pressure, and the oceans respond by making tides, which facilitates life in the ocean by stirring the water.

It is estimated that it takes 100 years for water in Antarctica to reach the Arctic Ocean. Everything has a sequence and purpose. It didn't surprise me to learn that scientists saw a black hole dismantle a star last August. One must realize that space moves electrons, and a vortex of space simply dissolves any atom and electron made material; it would be like running into a buzz saw. How many people realize that space is composed of currents similar to the actions of our oceans, or that our whole solar system is being carried along in one?

If we could observe tornados from outer space, we would see them as vortexes of air. When hot air rises, it creates an updraft, and the spinning of our Earth could be what gives them so much power.

Space is of such a fine viscosity that it doesn't move our air masses rapidly, even though we have a jet stream moving our weather patterns and affecting the flight of aircraft, which I suspect is affected by our Earth's rotation. After having prayed for wisdom and getting all these thoughts in my head, I've wondered if I was given a gift of discernment even so. As a human, my discernment can't help but have flaws in it, as has every theory proposed by many others up to now. I mentioned earlier that I thought permanent magnetism to be an eddy current of space, and I expect one to be an example of the activity surrounding each atom. Can you imagine how strong the cohesion between the atoms and electrons are in a diamond? The effect has to be immense to retain that hardness, and yet when a laser is used to drill holes in a gem, if the holes are near each other, they will join and make a single hole. Incredible!

Magnetism appears to be space in motion, and a permanent magnet exhibits a direct current effect. Therefore I have wondered if we could find a way to cause the magnetism to oscillate at the frequency of light, giving many people illumination for a small cost. LEDs are a huge help in creating light with small electrical input, and even though the compact fluorescents are efficient, they produce a lot of magnetic radiation, which has proved to be detrimental to our health as an aging effect. We have already found ways to improve loud speakers and electric motors so that they perform equally well with less power input by using permanent magnets in their field circuit, negating the need for field coils of wire that require as much energy to make the magnetic field as is required by the armature. Permanent magnets are also used in microwave ovens, suggesting that lights could be more efficient if we can find out how to use permanent magnets there as well.

Permanent magnets don't seem to exhibit any negative health effects and are even used medicinally. It doesn't seem to matter whether we move a magnet across a coil or a coil across a magnet—electrons are moved in the coil. A gauss meter measures the intensity of a magnet by placing a ribbon of metal carrying a direct current in the gap between the poles of the magnet and measuring the intensity by the amount of deflection of the current created by the magnetic flux, but neither direct current nor permanent magnetism can create transformer action; there has to be vibrating impulses to accomplish a change. When magnetism can affect the movement of electrons, it stands to reason that electrons travelling in a propeller-shaped ribbon; if rotated, could cause a draft of space movement, of propulsion, providing the metal is near the capacity flow of electrons to retain wave form.

For years I have wondered why other people have not come up with the ideas I have been writing down, and after asking Google on my computer about my idea of push gravity, I received information from Wikipedia in April of this year that says Le Sage's theory of gravitation is a kinetic theory of gravity originally proposed by Nicolas Fatio de Duillier in 1690 and later by Georges-Louis Le Sage in 1748. The theory proposed a mechanical explanation for Newton's gravitational force in terms of streams of tiny unseen particles (which Le Sage called ultra-mundane corpuscules) impacting all material objects from all directions. I surmised that it is the waves of energy from the many stars that act in like manner, travelling in straight lines from all directions, they seem concentrated in straight lines by adjacent

beams. You could see this effect by placing two magnets on a flat surface and using iron metal filings, where the fields touch, you will see a straight line. The light beams act similarly, and strike all objects from all sides, pressing against every object in our universe. However, instead of corpuscles I expect it to be the electrons formed from God partricles which I call magnetons because their flow gives us our magnetic effects. I find Le Sage's insight amazing in comprehending quite well what is actually happening without the benefit of today's findings in radio and atomic research. I earlier likened an electron to be like an ice cube in water. The ice cube is water in a solid form and can obstruct water movement, or it can move water when it is moved. An electron is apparently made from compacted space particles in suns; likewise, though made of space, it is opaque to space. When it is moved, it pushes on electrons so that when magnetism (a draft of space) is moved past anything made of electrons, the electrons are moved according to the intensity of the draft. It creates transformer action when in coils of wire and wound around an iron framework.

For some reason I haven't fathomed yet, iron facilitates this movement, as well as certain combinations of other metals, and I've wondered if the spacing between the atoms and electrons are acting in a capillary manner. There is simply no end to the wonders in God's creations.

After what I had previously deduced, I expected that if two electrons were floating in space, they would be pushed toward each other by the star waves coming in opposing directions. This seems to be what happens to immense gas clouds in space when space's infinite pressure causes an explosion, producing new planets—the Big Bang, which some assumed created our world billions of years ago.

Finding that Le Sage had deduced the push theory without our later findings gives me an emotional boost. He also felt we must be under pressure, and the knowledge has been out there for centuries, but our own fear of the unknown has prevented us from accepting "old" knowledge that is new to us. Years ago when working in the paint shop of an auto body garage, I saw what I later felt was an indication of gravity on the paint stir sticks. Before leaving the shop each night, we placed them in a container of lacquer thinners. In the morning the pigment would be evenly surrounding each one to the level of the fluid, whether it was made of metal or wood. The particles of pigment, after being dissolved, gravitated to the sides and were carried by horizontal gravity waves from all directions. I saw a similar effect on the stems of plants in quiet areas on the sides of ponds.

Everything we see, feel or touch is relative to other things. Though there is no light or oxygen miles down in the ocean with tons of pressure per square inch, *National Geographic* photographed large clams and worms wiggling near a hot gas vent from the earth's core. Vegetation higher up on the ocean floor moves with the ripples in the water, and sea creatures see others at their level.

People can live at higher altitudes on mountains than would be possible at the same height above sea level in the open, because the mountain mass inhibits opposing star waves that hit the other side of the mountain so are able to hold the oxygen against the mountain side to a higher level. I'm aware that scientists will want to have my statements proven to their satisfaction, but at 88 and without sufficient funds, I have to leave further investigation to younger minds with more means.

When we get to the heart of creation, we are entering the spiritual realm, and fathoming spiritual things requires us to be given spiritual discernment—a faith in things unseen, related to a few with an ability to believe that anything created has to have a planner with insight to what is needed and how to fashion it into a useful object.

The one we call God has done that millions of times, and He has given His human beings knowledge and resources in order to give them ways to enjoy beauty in all its facets. However, it requires us to obey His instructions by cooperating with each other for our mutual good, which is pleasing to Him when we realize that all these wonderful things were designed for our sustenance and enjoyment, and are obtainable to those who will obey God. Obedience is the key to open the door to joy.

The conclusions I have reached have come from a lifetime of observation at a hobby level; much of what I have written here will prove to be basically accurate, but it may not be accepted during my lifetime.

Galileo was severely persecuted for not accepting the view of the Roman Catholic Church leaders, who believed that the sun circled around the earth. Copernicus believed Galileo but kept quiet about it.

Newton assumed that if he doubled the speed of an object, it would double its impact. A woman mathematician proved that when you double the speed, you quadruple the impact, and some say it's eight times.

Benjamin Franklin assumed that the pole he named positive had a surplus of electrons, but the actual movement (as proved in vacuum tubes) was that it was the negative pole with the surplus. We have to give Albert Einstein credit for opening the door to a whole new era, but he paused on the threshold. All the past scientists and inventors have increased our knowledge immensely and deserve our admiration and appreciation for their patience and dedication over many years and difficult times.

, Our radio and atomic research fills in the blanks. If others can believe what I think of as my God-given theory, new inventions are sure to follow.

Madame Currie and her husband made a phenomenal discovery, opening our eyes to the world of the atom at a huge price to their health from not knowing the effects of radiation.

None of this would be possible without knowledge coming from God. If we want to know how something is made, we need to go to its creator. Revealing the truth about the actual nature of gravity can not only help us on Earth, but it could help to make space travel more accessible by knowing what we are dealing with. Seeing more of God's handiwork gives us a deeper respect for all creation.

My assumptions could be read as science fiction, which often becomes true later. Dick Tracy comics had wrist radios long before we had the ability to produce any. My theory will have flaws in it, but by analyzing it, new findings are sure to be revealed.

This message is an extension of what I wrote in my previous book, *The Way I See My God.* Much of it the same with new concepts added. I know that it is very difficult to accept that something that has been observed for hundreds of years has been based on a false premise, but this has occurred at different times in history.

This concept will be found true if my definition of gravity is accepted. Millions of calculations will still be valid, and previously missing pieces of the puzzle will be found. An example is solar flares: these are bursts of electrons expelled from the sun in shafts of immense energy. If you can accept that an electron is opaque to space, you will have some ability to see that the flare will push space ahead of it, and when this flow reaches our power lines, the electron flow of electricity can be disrupted. It has been so in the past when high-tension transformers have been burned out at power stations. The flare consists of high-frequency, direct current, and all electrons are negative. I mentioned this to a helicopter repair man, and he stated that this had happened in New Brunswick.

The scientific community can't have it both ways. To rationalize gravity as an attraction, Bob McDonald, a scientist on CBC, gave an answer to a "Quirks and Quarks" question from a viewer: "What pressure is there at the center of the earth?" McDonald stated, "Scientifically speaking, there isn't any." And yet huge gas clouds in space explode from pressure and make large explosions, creating new heavenly bodies. As I previously mentioned, miles down in the ocean the pressure can be tons per square inch. Everything is acting in a relative manner; volcanoes don't get sucked downward, and they act more like a safety valve on an automobile radiator. Molten lava exuding proves that the earth is hot at its core, and the lava is not radioactive, so the heat doesn't come from atomic power. If we will accept that God created everything from nought, my story will start to make sense.

What may be the hardest to grasp is that space behaves like a liquid under high pressure; its viscosity could be estimated by its speed of wave reaction, 186,300 miles per second, the speed of light. That's very fast, and yet it takes about 8 minutes for a wave of sunlight to reach our earth 930 billion, 200 million miles away. Our universe encompasses vast distances and immense power. Our sun sends out great clouds of electrons; it was noticed that the light from a star beyond the sun appeared to have its light bent, but with electrons from the sun creating a space wave ahead of it, pushing on the beam of ligt distorting it. This light beam from a star initiated by electron movement but made up of space would naturally be pushed aside, looking as if it had been bent until it appeared to snap when passing the sun. This relationship of electrons moving space and space moving electrons is fundamental to everything that has been created; power transformer action depends on it.

No human being will ever be able to determine where our God came from, or how space came into being, or whether we have one God in each planet, sun moon combination, our sky is full of them, but we worship one God.

What we conceive as space appears to be responding to, and is even dependent on, the cooperation of many other suns to create the lines of force making up the gravity that operates in everything, producing our weight, keeping things stabilized and pressing oxygen onto the Earth. This appears to be accomplished from the fact that electrons are opaque to space movement, so the beams of light made up of waves of space pulsating in the optical segment of the electromagnetic spectrum, will have an accumulated effect, and the deeper the layer of air, the higher the pressure becomes; with water and soil having many more electrons per cubic inch, the weight effect builds up rapidly. With more electrons that circle the nucleus of the atoms, the weight in each cubic inch increases. 14.7 pounds per square inch of air pressure at sea level builds to over 46,000 tons on an acre of land.

The latest huge accomplishment of the Curiosity Rover landing on Mars (August 6, 2012) makes me think that a lot of other people are aware of many of the ideas I've mentioned, but they are expressed in technical terms not previously well-known. They are to be congratulated for this major achievement, learning some more about the wonders of God's creation and hopefully having deeper respect for them.

The fact that the scientists at NASA were able to land a vehicle on Mars shows that whatever understanding they are using, they have an accurate grasp on how things are made, whether or not Newtonian theory is in it. Scientists need to be respected for all the advances that have occurred in knowledge, doing what I call an autopsy on the Earth and exposing how tiny the building blocks are, and how intricate everything is made and how vulnerable we are to actions of nature and our own mistakes. Archeology points to more than one previous civilization that has come and gone, leaving little for us to improve on. Expertise in moving huge weights and the precise cutting of blocks of stone are still mysteries, Stone Henge in England, on Easter Island in the South Pacific, pyramids in Egypt and South America, as well as space flight, ESP, divining of water and thought transmission over long distances. We have much to learn—and perhaps a limited time in which to start acting in a more altruistic manner. The Earth appears to have become somewhat unbalanced by the weight accumulation on our North and South poles by ice build-up, suggested by the alterations in our magnetic poles. They used to vary about five kilometers a year, but they are said to have wobbled about 50 kilometers in the direction of Siberia. As I mentioned earlier, farming occurred on Greenland between AD 800–1200, but increasing cold made it impossible to continue. The melting of the pole ice will relieve some of the imbalance by creating more water, which as a liquid will cause the planet to become more evenly balanced again, but much of the Earth will suffer greatly during this period from higher water levels worldwide. Our scientists are blaming our progress for causing the increase in heat, and to some degree this is true. Taking gas and oil from the Earth also allows heat from the center of the planet to escape to the surface by conduction. Water conducts much more heat than oil or gas, but this source appears to be ignored, as well as forest fires, which add to the gases. Our magnetism strength has been decreasing, and a shifting of the poles is possible.

Forest fires create a lot of gases; including carbon dioxide. Much of our lack of carbon disposal comes from eliminating the trees, which are our greatest carbon sinks. In spite of our self-blaming for warming, we fail to understand that though what we do is not helpful, the greater director of what will happen is in the purview of the one who made it all in the first place. We can improve our way of life by going back to the instructions that He gave us over 2,000 years ago on how to live successfully in His world.

Although space appears pure, it isn't. Atoms and electrons are floating in it and will be collected by being pushed toward any object that hinders the star wave vibrations from even a miniscule amount in a specific direction. The big explosions in space that create new heavenly bodies from collected gas clouds are adequate proof of it happening all the time. Our earth collects space dust constantly. Even a grain of sand requires a designer. It takes trillions of electrons to make one grain.

Mars may have gone through a tremendous upheaval, and instead of keeping it pure, we might be able to establish a living air around it by seeding it with various living bacteria, fungi and lichens, etc. It could take many years to establish new growing things to create oxygen sufficiently to bring in higher forms of life, but if we keep polluting our earth with atomic reactors, a new planet may be required for any form of humanity to continue at all. The possibility of us creating a nuclear disaster is very real. Heavy water—water with an added ion—comes out of the earth in some places naturally. His has occurred in Norway, and Hitler took the souce over hoping it could assist him in devising atomic bombs. England sent gliders pulled by bombers to try to eliminate this threat and lost a lot of good men in the attempt early in the second world war, I was a teen ager at the time. If ignited by a hydrogen bomb, the water on our earth could turn our earth into a new sun. Could it give life to Mars? This idea came from many sources over my lifetime. Not having kept a diary, I can't name a specific source, but I learned about this in the forties, but found it again on Google. This subject could make a book all by itself, there are also the residue of a Nuclear reactor; Look up, "Ancient reactor, Afrrica".

The Bible talks of the hills melting in the fervent heat, but does it have to happen? Is it up to us? What I've put together is a sketch/ I've left the intricate parts to the experts out of necessity.

Knowledge is life giving and saving, whereas ignorance can be fatal—and often is. The incredible advances in technology need not be for nothing; they could create a way for remnants of our civilization to start anew, perhaps on Mars, or can we start over again where we are, renouncing all forms of self-aggrandizement, caring for others and thereby assuring our own survival. At the least, we could create an improvement for whatever time our earth has left in this cycle. Our earth has been going through cycles for thousands of years. According to estimates by Dr. Paul LaViolette, they've been occurring on approximately 10,000–12,000 years apart, and we're almost due. The degeneration of our morality worldwide—with the abortion of so many precious souls, the lack of altruism and the legalization of wholesale exploitation of what is called "democratic free enterprise" looking more like legalized

Donald Dolson

stealing—has caused the need for food banks and created more homelessness. More burdens are on people with tender hearts, and it paints a picture of the second coming of Christ. I'm still working on this and really need someone more able to aid me. I believe the subject needs to be aired, and the need for godliness has never been more acute than it is right now. The Judeo-Christian Bible has our solution.

Chapter 3

Love and Some of Its Many Facets

When talking of God's love, it seems natural to me to discuss what He has given to humans. I speak from personal observation and experience from a Christian layman's perspective. Not having a license to counsel, I urge the reader to seek out whatever professional he or she prefers, perhaps remembering that professional courtesy has altered or suppressed some of the findings. Much of my information comes from personal experience and people like Theologian Dr. John Drakeford and his book *Integrity Therapy*, co-authored with Psychologist Dr. Hobart Mowerer, they promoted the highest integrity pointing out that each of us has a deep need to be personally responsible for our own actions, for our mental health and those around us. I also rely on many other professionals in other fields, our own discussion group in Toronto Single Parents for nearly ten years and personal contacts.

God's love is the most profound and the greatest, as proven by what He has given us beyond creating us and everything visible and invisible.

Love is a doing word, a "life of voluntary effort" for the sake of others. If followed by the majority, it gives most people a feeling of security and belonging cooperatively. Like priming a pump to get water, we have to give love to get love, and that means showing faith in others and being helpful wherever we can, when needed and when we have the ability.

True love is faith in its deepest form, a willingness to give even without a hope of getting. One might even call it a happy addiction because it doesn't always, if ever, follow one's intellect.

Some people feel they have to follow their feelings, not realizing that feeling good is the reward for doing and being good, from God's perspective. When you feel a respectful and deep affection, sexual attraction may not be noticeable if the problems of your friend are more important to you than your own at that time. Agape (spiritual love) conveys this attitude; I know it personally. We may feel warm in our genitals when holding a tiny baby or hugging someone, but this does not signal that we should get sexual satisfaction; this is a normal reaction in someone who has a caring feeling for others. Our whole bodies still have some primitive reactions for those unspeakable sensations. It's a privilege to have tender feelings, because they have appropriate channels. It is said that love makes the world go round, and at its most basic point, God's love does.

It is shown in everything we can see, feel or touch, and the motions are central to our existence, which requires His constant motivation to keep electrons rotating and maintain the atoms and integral parts that make everything into a recognizable reality.

In our physical selves, the will to procreate is considered next in strength to our will to live, and without its sequence there would have been no past, present or future for any human life. The rewards for engaging in the possibility of bringing a new human into this world to know love, and stand in awe at the wonders of God's creation and be prepared for another generation to continue the family, give us pleasure.

However, just as every seed that falls is not expected to produce new life, each moment of togetherness of a man and woman is more often a renewal of the feeling of affection and acknowledgement of their need for each other, a special bond of loyalty and respect.

When living is very stressful, at the subconscious level the need to reproduce feels imperative, and animals, people and even vegetation try to adapt to the need. This is often noticed in people in our armed services. The constant stress and uncertainty in their service duties makes them extra conscious. The Bible says that the greatest love is shown by those who give up their own lives for the sake of others, and many of them have done that. It is happening too often and is not fully appreciated by some people.

Christ is our best example in laying down His life for us. I felt as if I had fallen in love with the soloist in Fairbank Baptist Church in Toronto in 1967, during an Eric Richards Crusade, when I accepted Him as my saviour. I felt as if I had shed a heavy weight and was ecstatic after being depressed and hopeless. My feelings of self-condemnation for things slipping out of my hands, as well as my priorities, changed immediately and are still with me. I have a new reality and have found that I could voice my thoughts in poetry almost as easily as breathing. I knew it was His Holy Spirit when it was still with me after I got home from church. I am more deeply convinced than ever of His presence, even though I backslid later for a time, I was on the valium prescribed for my depression, which also lowered helpful inhibitions, making me more vulnerable to fleshly temptations. I lost my initial elation but found Him faithful when I repented and asked His forgiveness. Satan attacks as soon as we take a stand for Christ, and I was an easy target during my single-parent years, searching for a new mate. Thirteen years later it happened, I *had prayed for a godly wife* and we have been happily married for over 36 years.

In our Western world, we recognize three kinds of love: erotic (physical), familial (family), and agape (spiritual). If we have been fortunate enough to feel all three in a committed love relationship, a long and satisfying existence with the likelihood of having golden and possibly diamond wedding anniversaries is a realistic hope.

For it to be a reality, ideally we need to know God in our lives daily with gentle, positive mentoring, although others have succeeded even though faced with many difficulties. Both parents contribute. A respectful, gentle attitude between parents is noticed by children and is a pattern for what is considered as normal behaviour in a home setting. When little Johnny sees his mother's face light up when Dad gives her a hug or pat when he gets home from work, he wants to be like his dad. It requires more than just telling for a child to learn how to live; good examples are needed, and the more the better. People are tempted to do what they see and hear others doing around them, and a good home life where children know they can get positive help gives them the strength to withstand many of the temptations. Learning to say no to requests to do something that your parents say is wrong or could be harmful later helps children to be confident and responsible individuals. They find that others who have done the actions they were tempted to do, and did them even when told not to, have fared badly, reinforcing their convictions as to what is right or wrong.

Contrary to what is often said today, anything that you do that can harm you or others in some avoidable way, now or later, is definitely wrong for you, even if it has been legalized. An unwise decision based on feeling and without an intellectual verification can lead to life-long sorrow, as can be seen in the gay community. The gay lifestyle seems to appeal to the sensitive people who find the human race too daunting: artists, musicians, dancers, and Hedonists who are looking for a quick fix. In my single-parent years, I saw the collateral damage: some people become so depressed that they commit suicide, and others have nervous breakdowns when their spouse brings home a gay lover. I believe gays to be victims of a permissive society; so many people are busy just making a living that they don't notice their sons having fantasies, or if they do, they brush it off as a passing fancy, not realizing that "as the twig is bent, the tree is inclined." Gently giving him the normal expectations at that time will usually help him to turn his thoughts away from that angle of thinking. Proffessor Emeritus Donal De Marco of St. Geromes College at the University of Waterloo, gave the scientific reson that God says NO to homosexuality In THE INTERIM, page 24, April 2004, but the general public has not been warned of the danger through articles by other Christian leaders. This has left vulnerable youth in imminent poeril of being hooked by the most insidious addiction known to man. The

Canadian Government legalized it without a Referendum, and has brain washed a lot of society, not admitting that professional coutesy may have had a part. I published the whole sequence, and it was copyrighted in my book titled "It Could Help a Young Man to Know' in 2012 by Essence publishging. I had spent 23 years in the federal Liberal Party, mostly in policy at the local level, I was known by quite a few people, I took photos at conventions, I was called their conscience and their poet, but I left when homosexuality was legalized, and abortion.

As a sickly child because of undiagnosed lactose intolerance, I was alone a lot and had times of feeling lonely, no friends at school, rejected because of a health problem giving me an unpleasant odour, and I could feel affection for anyone who made me feel I was accepted and respected. With godly parents, straight brothers, and no gay friends, I outgrew tempting feelings and aimed my romantic feelings at young ladies. All addictions have a portion of love feeling in them; it acts as a hook, and we're trying to find a way to feel we belong to one individual or to a group. It's a kind of hunger, and some people eat to try to feel fulfilled. Others take to smoking, drinking or taking drugs, but they are all escape mechanisms being used to make people feel better.

When my first wife died from a car accident I went into depression and was prescribed Valium as part of my treatment. It relieved that feeling of having the Grand Canyon in my chest, but I was on it too long and finally realized that it also took away some helpful inhibitions that were meant to keep me from having more woe or hurting others. Years later I kicked it with difficulty. The old feelings came back for a while, but I decided I would not let a chemical dictate my life and gave myself permission to change my attitude. No one else could do it for me. We have the responsibility of directing our own lifestyles. Our physical bodies have minds of their own. I think of it as ancient wisdom. Even when the spinal cord is disrupted, this ancient wisdom keeps healing physical injuries to the unfeeling body. This may explain to some degree why acupuncture works, when insecurity or fear in our minds send out panic signals, preventing an accent on natural healing. In first aid, a simple example is when we accidently hit our thumb with a hammer; if we do nothing, a blood blister is apt to form from a panic reaction increasing blood pressure there temporarily, but if we choke it with our other hand for a few minutes, the panic subsides, and although tender, the thumb heals well with no blood blister.

Unfortunately there are few remedies for severely disappointed or bruised feelings, or broken hearts although surrendering to Christ has been a lifesaver in more ways than one. His ability to help us to let go of the past and start over fresh has renewed our hopes and relieved our guilt.

A Broken Heart

Some say a broken heart that mends
can't be broken again,
That it becomes tough and bitter to the core.
Before you take your life and end it,
give Christ a chance to mend it.
He can make it better than before.

Mothers are more in tune with daughters, but boys often need a conscientious dad to know best what he needs to learn, because Dad knows more of how boys think and feel. Much of this was lost in the first World War, when dads went overseas, mothers worked in factories and children were given a quarter to go and see movies, which became their source of information on how to live. This deficit of godly example was compounded by the Second World War, when adults without sufficient examples themselves had children. We see the results today: an increase in divorces, broken hearts and homes, unwed mothers, a burgeoning social service and moral decline. My Scotch great-grandmother (likely Presbyterian) married a Roman-Catholic man, and they had two daughters before breaking up. He took one daughter and seemed to disappear; my grandmother stayed with my great-grandmother and felt rejected because her mother pined for her other daughter without noticing that the one she still had longed for affection. When grown, Grandmother went to the United States and married my mother's father, though she still missed her own mother. This is one example; and it is repeated many times in society and needs to be recognized.

This unrequited love is experienced by anyone who has genuinely loved and been rejected for whatever reason. Even without any enmity, that longing can haunt someone for a lifetime. There is this indefinable area of connection, seemingly not recognized by many people of a spiritual connection, but most noticeable in animals and birds and even fish, where they feel compelled to return to that original place where they felt they belonged, where their original seed had been planted and started to grow. Adopted children and even in-vitro ones have shown this feeling of a need to know their roots. Many people have remarked that it seemed as though God had left such a place in the human psyche that only He can fill. This has been recognized especially in primitive people when understanding John 3:16–17. Some people have been so convinced that they will give up their lives rather than be taken from this realization. Although it is good to know about the one you love, you don't need to know everything if your conviction is real, even though some people seem to feel they have to read the whole Bible and be constantly embroiled in Bible studies to feel fully committed. Billy Graham has no theological degree (he went to Wheaton College and Florida Bible Institute), but by simply believing in God and by telling it to the world, he has been of help to millions of people. We enjoy reading his "Decision" magazine. Today's unspoken attitude in the religious community suggests that we need to study the Bible and follow the higher level of understanding in order to ensure our future in heaven. Jesus faulted the scribes and Pharisees of His day for putting on so many regulations beyond what people could bear. He called them "White-washed sepulchres" and proceeded to show the simplicity of faith.

C. S. Lewis, a highly educated man and one time an atheist, turned to Christ and felt compelled to bring the Gospel into the area of those in lower and middle classes, seemingly deserted by what looks like an elitist part of society with their own language of complicated words. Even though I was raised in a godly family, and I heard many sermons, I still found it confusing when, to gather for a rest period, it's called a retreat, and an extensive study about God and divine things is called theology. Then there is eschatology, a study pertaining to theological studies, and we have apologetics, a defensive method of arguing to justify Christian belief. To me, it's something to be proud of, and I feel the title is misleading. Another is ecclesiastical, pertaining to the church and its preachers. Why don't we just say so? In my opinion, it's no wonder so many churches are empty, because for those unfamiliar with this branch of learning it can be daunting. The rest of life is so busy that learning another language in order to know what the pastor is talking about doesn't seem worth it. To be truly helpful, Christians need to admit that God's word does require reverence and is not looked upon as a social group governed by a committee that can change the rules. In order to be truly helpful, we have to realize that God's laws were made to help us. Too many pastors appear to lean on the guilt button without pointing out the reason God sent us His son, or why He died for us.

Many people are already aware of a sense of worthlessness; they need to be lovingly put back on the road to salvation, which is the example Jesus gave us. Our mother learned to read, sing, and play music on the organ or piano, but she couldn't play by ear. Her son Boyd learned to read music, but he preferred to play from memory. Mother had played the organ and sang in her father's church.

Exercising our faith can make a long, tedious, critical evaluation of each verse unnecessary, by remembering that all the material that we can read has been put together by imperfect people, even though they are supposed to be "God breathed." The Bible says, "There are no righteous, no not one!" except Jesus Christ Himself, and He didn't publish the Bible or anything else. Faith is not dependant on feelings; it is an unspoken conviction in the back of our minds and hearts that stays in spite of variations in feelings. If you read a portion of scripture that is opposite to what God has given to you in love, believe the one that constantly affirms the love and caring of our heavenly father. He wants us to treat each other like brothers and sisters, and we should treat others in the way we want to be treated ourselves. Some people do feel a need to dwell on the Bible, and if you've learned something of counselling, you know that if a person wants to talk about things (the Bible especially). they need a sympathetic ear. For them it is a need to be respected; they may simply need to have more information.

God is love! With a deep care for each of us, He gives us ample opportunities to ask forgiveness and is merciful. He is also strict, and so we must be saved in order to enter His home; no rebels will be there.

PEOPLE

People need people; our hearts need a song.
Everyone needs to feel they belong,
To know what God's love is, the deep pleasure of giving.
This gift is His and brings meaning to living.
A cheery hello as we go on our way
Could help someone to know a much pleasanter day.
A pat on the back may be all that it takes
To fill a deep lack, or to ease a heartache.
"Thank you so much," we all like to be told;

It's the sort of soft touch that makes
out world seem less cold.
Each kindness performed is a gift from above,
And our lives are transformed by the power of love.

I see my God as the greatest father figure ever. Many
people insist that our obedience is strictly to give God all
the glory, that He wants compliance to gratify only Himself.
I see that attitude as a human failing. If we look at all He has
done to make our lives possible, we can see that His greatest
concern is for us to live long happy, healthy, guilt-free
lives, and He is exalted when we understand and give Him
our gratitude, even though we can feel that our ability to
really show Him sufficient appreciation is very inadequate.
Having made us, He knows our every weakness, and He
gave us His Ten Commandments as guard rails on our road
of life, as well as added reminders from the prophets and
in Jesus's words. If followed, they assure us of a favourable
outcome. Knowing we might fail, He has given us means to
be forgiven and start over. By sending Jesus to show us how
to live, He even had Him die so that God could prove that He
knew every feeling any of His created beings could possibly
have. I heard a theologian state, "We're not under the law
anymore, but under grace." That is true, but Christ said,
"I came to fulfil the law," and He did. He became a human
sacrifice to prove how deeply our heavenly father actually
cares for us. We as humans lack the ability to praise God
as much as He deserves; we can only give Him all we are,
and that is pleasing to Him. His actions proved to everyone
willing to read it that God is in connection with His son
and felt all the feelings He experienced when Christ was

crucified, as well as all of what we experience. That fact should make people aware that God does know, and He has made allowances for each and every failing so that we can be saved if we are willing to follow His directions.

We do need to read our Bibles, with the fewer translations the better; we are exposed to too many watered-down versions that not only permit but encourage selfish behaviour. When we pay attention to the first two commandments and realize that if most people are able and willing to think of others, everyone is safer, then there is no need for so much homelessness or so many food banks and jails. God didn't give any human being the right to alter any of His laws. Anyone using His name to bless an action He has banned is taking God's name in vain and will not be deemed guiltless. His laws are life saving and life giving, whereas ignorance can be and often is fatal.

The Hope Peddler

Did you know that our pastor's a pusher?
That the Bible contains all his dope?
That he's asked the congregation and
ushers to help him peddle hope?
He's after everyone in his region; he
wants us to get the church habit.
He thinks when it comes to religion,
everyone should be an addict.
Nowhere else can we get the right
fix for all our emotional ills.
God cures a heart that is sick better than all of our pills.

When we drink at His fountain, we
can be intoxicated with love,
Have faith to climb any mountain,
and hope for heaven above.
When we drink one of our potions, we
may not know where we're at.
God fills lives with love and devotion—
no drug on earth can do that.
Our smiles can be contagious when
we've been injected with grace.
Some say these claims are outrageous, but
His power can be seen every place,
For when we have no hope of winning,
we've lost all our fair-weather friends.
If we ask, we'll find as in the beginning
that God is still there at the end.

Jews were more advanced in this area centuries ago, and wings on hospitals testify to their ongoing concern for societies' well-being with their number of philanthropies.

God showed His forgiving love long before Christ was born, in the story of Moses, who was programmed from birth to do a great service for the Jewish people. He learned the Arabic language and all their cultural ways when brought up as a son of the Pharaoh's daughter.

Even though he killed an Egyptian who had been abusing a Jewish slave and hid on the far side of a desert, God used him to lead the Jews out of Egypt and bring us the Ten Commandments. He was considered to be esteemed by God. God forgives even murder if we repent and go back to Him. In his youth, King David killed Goliath, the giant

Philistine who had been threatening the Jews, and David became a hero. Later as king, he seduced Bathsheba and had her soldier husband killed in battle, but when Nathan the prophet accused him, over time he became so conscience stricken that he wrote the Psalms, which have been a comfort to millions of people for thousands of years. It was from the line of David that Jesus appeared. God covered all the bases in His efforts to assure the maximum number of His children to be saved.

If a majority of birds, animals or people become so competitive as to be seen as predatory, their own existence becomes in jeopardy. Symptoms are showing already in our society: our young are not well planned in, and we are not replacing our population. Realty's efficiency has made home owning and family raising too difficult for the majority of children from early pioneer Canadians. Governments are often more charitable to newcomers, giving them more freedom of religion and living space while curtailing those of early Canadians who made freedom possible at considerable cost to themselves. These descendants feel it as a betrayal by the prime ministers who seem more concerned with winning power than in showing loyalty to the people they are elected to serve—people who sacrificed a great deal to get us our freedom of speech and religion. Canada's foundation was that of a Christian nation, and it was peaceful, with concern and respect for all who would reciprocate; that was our rightful expectation.

Many early pioneers came to Canada and the United States to escape the religious persecution they had endured in Europe. Before the Trudeau and Chretien eras, Canada had earned the reputation of being the best place in our world to live because of early Canadian values based on God's laws and godly living. Some people today talk of "Canadian values," but they don't look much like the ones I learned 60 or 70 years ago; they've been legally warped to accommodate the feelings of a minority who disdain heterosexuality. Other people came after most of the hard work had been done by the pioneers, but they have brought with them their old attitudes from other parts of the world. They take advantage of our freedom of worship, but they don't reciprocate.

My great, great, great grandfather came to Canada in 1812 at 12 years of age with three older brothers. The family settled near Georgetown, Ontario. One brother went to Niagara, another went to near Simcoe, and one stayed in what is called Georgetown, possibly with our ancestor.

Trudeau legalized homosexuality between adults and brought multiculturalism to Canada. Gays sued the government to have their rights put into the constitution, and Jean Chretien put secular judges on the Supreme Court who deferred to the demands of gays.

The new law made it illegal for anyone to oppose it,. A parent or teacher can be prosecuted in Canada for trying to keep a child from going gay. We mustn't be homophobic; instead, we make them victims of lust, letting them opt out of the human race. Legality has usurped the role of justice and common sense. Even though homosexuality can spread through thought, word and deed, it hasn't been classed as an addiction, and those who become hooked ought to be treated as victims and given the kind of concern we show for those who have fallen prey to Satan's wiles. They should be treated as victims of a permissive society, as we do for alcoholics and heroin addicts. Once addicted, it becomes very difficult to change, because each addiction seems to mimic in some way a comforting feeling similar to a love or relief, even if for a short time. These addictions add more problems to other parts of our society. I backslid in other ways for a time after my conversion, but I asked God for forgiveness, and though I lost my initial exuberance I had felt when I first accepted Him in 1967, I have become more convinced than ever of His forgiveness, having experienced how subtly we can be taken in by Satan's wiles.

Psychologists and psychiatrists are well aware that we can steer our thoughts in almost any direction we want to go, and we rationalize and justify our choices through repetition. Other people deserve concern, but the majority prefer to be heterosexual. Why, in a democracy, should they be forced to bow to the wishes of those who have chosen to plant their seeds in a waste container, avoiding personal obligations for momentary pleasure, even if it does give them a high? If a same-sex spouse dies, taxpayers are billed for spousal allowance even when they haven't contributed as a mother could. Even without children, a woman has gifts to share that he doesn't possess, and she is an appropriate example for other children.

It is also goes against the will of God, who wants us to have what is best for us all, with the feelings that provide the ability and motivation to reproduce progeny in a God-approved fashion, with the opposite sexes using their special gifts to help each other. If people claiming to be Christian church members were fully committed, there would be no schisms, and societal problems would be cared for where needed. Studies have shown that some people do have hereditary genes that make them less able to withstand temptation, but to say "God made gays to be that way" denies our ability to learn or to be taught right from wrong.

Professor emeritus, Donald DeMarco at the University at St. Jeromes College at The University of waterloo, wrote an article for The Interim, page 24, April, 2004. "What science tells us of "same sex unions". He gives a scientific run down of the whole subject, explaining the way it is dangerous for the health of each participant.

His explanation shows why God says "NO".God loves us.
His accomplishments are on your computer.

Try to read Elain Aron's book *HSPs: Highly Sensitive People.* It's a helpful eye opener. She estimates that society has about 20 percent highly sensitive people, over 40 percent not sensitive, and the rest with varying degrees covering a wide variety of ways. This explained to me what I had seen during my nearly ten years in Single Parents Associated: some people regained their composure much more quickly than others after a devastating loss.

Coal-burning plants are being eliminated in Canada because they produce a large number of pollutants, but if we were to spend the kind of money that is necessary to operate atomic power plants on cleaning up coal-burning operations through using waterfalls, static and catalytic converters and whatever else is necessary, coal could give us power for many years to come without the danger created by the use of atomic power. Coal does not create atomic radiation while being operated or in storage. We would have little pollution without the danger of residual radiation during operation, from spent fuel rods that are very difficult to safely store. Once initiated; the atomic reaction can continue for thousands of years, the radiation erodes any container. Why can't we convert that atomic radiation into electricity similar to using solar cells? Radiation from power plants poisons air for many miles beyond, even though it may not be easily detected; cancers occur years later, hundreds of miles away.

An atomic scientist working on the atom bomb testing in Nevada suggested a certain number of increased leukemia cases in New York City, and he was labeled a fear monger, but years later his numbers were much too low—it was worse than he'd anticipated.

We know that trees are our greatest carbon sinks: they absorb carbon dioxide and put out oxygen into our air. We need to plant millions more, instead of denuding our landscape with clear cuts or any other operation that cuts more down than can be replaced. Trees need to do their job of clearing up pollution, and they require considerable time to grow in order to be effective.

Love is notably absent at present; it is usually proven by our actions of helping each other.

Every time we say no to something not quite right, we strengthen our will power, just like using a muscle to strengthen it for whatever chores we have to do. In time it becomes natural, and friends know not to ask us to take drugs or alcohol, or to go to wild parties. A deeper satisfaction comes from doing what God says is right; you can respect yourself when you do.

It doesn't seem usual for some people to recognize that love is shown by what we do. A woman does it when washing floors, getting meals, tending children or in any number of ways. A man can do it by persevering in a host of stressful jobs in order to support his family, or in doing jobs needed to be done in the community. Some jobs can be thankless and frustrating, or even dangerous, but they are still necessary, like working on high-voltage lines or in tunnels. An understanding spouse can make it all seem worthwhile. The noblest of carreers, the "Homemaker".

An Overworked Woman

I've given up my youth and looks; I've
toiled my whole life through.
I've washed and sewed, ironed and
cooked, half of the night-time, too.
Now I'm feeling really tired, but I don't mind too much.
But I do need someone near me who
can thrill me with his touch.
Life can't be all work, eat and sleep;
there must be more than that.
I have some feelings that are deep,
but I don't even get a pat.
I don't expect to be admired or kept in ecstasy,
But now I'm feeling really tired, I
need someone just for me.
I need someone who really understands;
whom I can look up to with pride.
When I feel like a frump with no appeal,
it's because love has been denied.

These attitudes are all too often carried into personal relationships; immediate gratification has become aggrandized even though the results can be seen as harmful, as can be seen in legalized abortion. God has supplied that union of sperm and egg with the spirit of life, and within 10–12 weeks the tiny heart, with an electrical impulse from its sinus node, will start pumping blood through its tiny body, possibly for the next hundred years. As its ears and brain develops, it will learn to recognize its parents' voices and be influenced by music played within hearing distance from the vibrations coming into the mother's tummy. It wants to live and has a right to expect that it will be welcomed. It didn't ask to be born—two people put in their order, which in nature is recognized as a promise, a marriage. When an abortion is used for convenience, those responsible are showing contempt for God's greatest gift, breaking a solemn promise by taking an innocent life. The woman has that knowledge in the back of her mind, and it can haunt her all her life; some women are unable to have a child later, and that is a high price to pay.

God did not abhor the Virgin's womb; neither should any man if he hopes to please God.

If a Fetus Could Speak

My arrival is supposed to bring gladness,
something the whole family enjoys.
I was never meant to bring sadness,
whether I'm a girl or a boy.
I'm a bundle full of potential, of hope, joy and much else.

> If you want to see what I could be, you
> only have to look at yourself.
> I'm programmed to have many of your
> features: my skin, my hair and my eyes.
> I'm a complicated affectionate creature
> who could be like you, even in size.
> If you don't want me, don't put in your
> order; I only come on command.
> I don't want to be an abortion after
> my lifetime's been planned.

In the animals and birds, the sexual mating is the marriage contract, and this used to be accepted by Jews. There were three ways a man could get a Jewish wife: buy her from her father, make their promises in front of a rabbi, or through sexual intercourse she says okay with her body and is the one who will have the most responsibility and effect in the life of her child. Her womb was necessary for its existence, and in her mind the child is an extension of herself. The mother determines the race or religious aspect by the Jews because the father may not always be there, but the mother is definitely present.

Love and pain are familiar cousins; one seldom exists without the other in the emotional part of our existence. Although love has been given three basic types, pain has been estimated in a range of 1–10, with 10 being considered the most severe. Each of us has a different range of perception, so what one person considers a 10 may be barely noticed by a person who is endowed with a much less sensitive physique. But being less sensitive physically does not mean the same person will be callous emotionally. Each of us is unique. Someone very sensitive to personal things can be uncaring to others, but each of us can change with an alteration in our environment or by giving ourselves permission to change our attitudes; no one can do it for us.

Tragedies affect people differently. One person loses a mate and becomes hard and bitter toward others, and even angry towards God. Perhaps is jealous of someone with a mate. However, someone else in a similar situation becomes more gentle and considerate toward others, and she can even feel glad to see other people in a happy marriage or in the birth of a baby, even though her own died.

This can be seen often when the person is at peace within himself or herself. Many people have found their inner peace through their faith in Jesus Christ, believing that He paid for their mistakes by sacrificing Himself after giving us His example on how to live with others. It's not always easy and can take many years to relinquish self-expectations. This happened to me through tragedies. I think that being born somewhat timid made it easier, but I know I can never be perfect—if I was, I wouldn't need a saviour. Christ came to save sinners, and I qualify.

As I mentioned already, we have these different levels, three for love and ten for pain, but I find these figures inadequate. The degrees and types of the individual facets of either one could go into the hundreds, and the levels are constantly changing in our lives, depending on personal health and environment. I am sure this has been noticed by many, and words are often inadequate to describe what and how we feel, because feelings can be complex from several angles at once. We call the sudden attraction to someone an infatuation even though the same initial feeling can turn into a genuine love bond over time. I learned that the only people who have the opportunity to actually know how grief-stricken people feel are people who have experienced the situation themselves. Some expert professionals are often unable to be really helpful if they lack personal experience and are not sensitive people to start with. That is why AA and single-parent clubs appear to have more success with some of their members, even though they may not be recognized by some professionals, whose egos from "higher learning" may preclude their admitting that someone else is actually more knowledgeable and helpful than they are. I've spoken to exceptions whose training gave them a better advantage in comforting people. Being open and honest works well many times, but there are times when it is best to be quiet because we can't really know how the other person feels or why; the situations are too numerous. Sometimes the most love can be shown just by being there and being willing to get a needed object. (A man from my church did that for me when Mary died.)

I read a story about a little boy who was 4 years old and went next door to a neighbour who had lost his wife. They boy sat on his lap, and when he came back his mother asked him, "What did you say?"

He said, "I didn't say anything. I just helped him cry." That says it all: the boy didn't know it, but tears help to carry away the negative substances created by grief, I do have moments of reflection where I see where I missed out on opportunities that could have changed my whole future, but it seems to me that my life happened the way it did so that I could learn what I needed to know and what to do to fit into what God had planned for my future. This book is one of them. It seems that it can take a lifetime to realize that God has been steering your life, even when you feel you have goofed up and could have done better. He takes what is there and uses our mistakes as training sessions; He is able to make something good or helpful from the worst possible situations.

God's main concern seems to be our spirits, and after having made them to start with, He will take them back and care for them. A tombstone read, "To be with Christ, which is far better." I was struck numb after Mary died from being struck by a car. I felt like going after the young driver, but the words in our "Lord's prayer" hit me like a club: "Forgive us our trespasses, as we forgive those who trespass against us." It took years for the feeling to disappear, but it did, and I concluded that God is more interested in our spirits; He will care for them. If He were to stop all our mistakes, He would be denying us our free will, and He can't be untrue to Himself. God gave us our spirits and will care for them when they return home. I see people as spirits clothed in flesh to enjoy His many wonders, and to be thankful.

The whole spiritual world is one of subtle mystery, using a means of communication not dependent on electrical means and yet known by animals, birds, fish and sensitive human beings through what is called extrasensory perception. I've experienced ESP more than once, but it is not a faculty that I can call upon, or depend on; it's elusive, and there were times when I didn't know my hunch was correct until later. I met a woman at a single-parent dance whom I wanted to date, and we had one pleasant date at a religious meeting. Although I talked to her quite a few times, she didn't consider me to be in her social class, but there were occasions when I felt she was leaving home to come to a dance at the Timothy Eaton Memorial Church in Toronto, and I sensed when she was in the back of the hall sometimes. Still, we never got close. Years later I met my second wife, Ruth, there. I've had similar experiences of ESP over the years, so for me ESP is a reality and is commonly recognized among natives in primitive countries.

In a book by Catherine Marshall, *Beyond Ourselves*, (The wife of Peter Marshall, former chaplain to a U.S. president) she was widowed, and mentions what happened on a talking tour. She stayed overnight in that city and dreamed of travelling in an automobile down a street where the houses were quite distinct in their appearance. When nearing a corner, a truck suddenly appeared in their lane. The following day, while travelling in a car going to the meeting, she was surprised while looking out the window to see what looked like the same houses she had seen in her dream. She asked her driver to pull over just as they were nearing a corner, and a truck came into view in their lane—just as she had seen in her dream. These things do happen, but we don't always get warned in time. In Bible times these happenings would be called prophetic and would be accepted as such. Today, we pay no heed, calling it a coincidence. A *Reader's Digest* remarked, "God works hard to make coincidences happen." For most things there is a cause and effect; so why is God concerned with little things but does not stop huge tragedies from happening? God has stepped in many times unobtrusively to lessen the severity of accidents; people survive sometimes when there seems no possibility that anyone could have, and if people are taken, their spirits remain in good hands. I've had proof of His physically saving me several times when no one else was present. One time I was going to have a bath and slipped, crashing my head so hard on the wall that Ruth heard me in the kitchen, the remarkable thing is that I didn't get any kind of bump or bruise, not even a tenderness. I thought, "God you must be saving me for something, it was repeated, same result"

That seemed uncanny, but life has no guarantees. A pot can't criticize the potter, and what happens can be foreordained as the life of Christ was. In His human body He expressed a wish to go on living in the Garden, where He prayed shedding drops of blood, but God went to the extreme in order to save His created beings. That shows how great His love is. We have been reticent in accepting His directions for a long, satisfying, guilt-free life. I didn't say "happy" because this is up to us: how and what we allow ourselves to think determines what we are going to feel or do, to some extent. Our bodies are often more honest than our minds.

You could be a businessman, and you may want to have a young pretty secretary with the ability of twenty years of experience. A woman sees a good-looking guy and tries to look her prettiest, but he's a working man not at her social level, and her heart isn't in it. She can be pleasant, but her body isn't interested; her main need is a feeling of security for anything permanent. However, as we've seen in TV shows, if a guy has a large house and expensive car, she can convince herself that he is lovable, but the marriage often doesn't last. I saw it repeated in the single-parent scene, where people focused their attention on immediate gratification. Just imagine her body talking: "How does she expect me to warm up to him when she doesn't respect him as a person?" After years in the club, it was like watching a play. The actors kept changing, but the sequence remained the same, hoping people could change to suit them but failing more often than not. We can only change ourselves; with God's help, we have to give ourselves permission to alter our attitudes because no one else can.

Reciprocal Love

Love is the outpouring of the faith in each of us.
Our faith is built up by the ones we've learned to trust.
When we say what we will do and do the things we say,
People learn to trust us as we live from day to day.
If we can learn to trust each other, we
may find a love that's true.
The love you show to me comes
from the faith I have in you.
I think that it is lovely, for it isn't hard to see
The faith I have in you came from the way you trusted me.

That is God's way of acting, too. He first of all made a way and place for us to live, in a Garden with all that we needed, but we chose to exercise our free will in a negative fashion, bringing down God's judgment, (disobedience is sin) and the whole sequence of what has happened since. However, He also made provisions for us to be rehabilitated and acceptable to His kingdom, and His offer still remains. Read your Bible carefully and take into consideration that our creator only wants what is best for us. Believe it and act accordingly, in order to help yourself and others.

So what has all this have to do with the greatest love ever shown? The depth of our love is shown in what we do; by our fruits we are known, and God has shown us the most fruits in what is evident now. He spent billions of our years (according to what geologists have discovered in the Earth) in order to make our world habitable. The first civilization of humans in some ways, was more advanced than we are now in some of their abilities, according to the huge stones neatly cut and fitted, as well as curious structures, pyramids and other structures and remnants still here: Stonehenge, (England) Easter Island heads,(South Pacific) the Pyramids in (Egypt and in South America). Amazing relics

Loving means caring, so do all you can for your God, for your family and for your fellow man. In doing so, we are following the example given to us by God.

Human feelings vary, as I've already mentioned. Unfortunately erotic feelings are so intimate that some people, unable to find the proper words, put it into the category of something dirty, when it is meant to be very beautiful and bring out our most noble feelings.

The Bible puts it another way and says, "His bowels yearned for the person." (Love is a hunger alright)

The same thing can happen when dancing with the opposite sex, but when fulfilment is not expected or wanted, our bodies can become adjusted and not excited in that situation. This adjustment takes nothing away from our ability to perform in a marital situation. You might call it a physical education that could make a young man able to act in a truly gentlemanly way, with less chance of causing embarrassment in a social setting. When a couple gets married, children are a possible expectation, but she may find that when nursing a baby, it can be so satisfying to her that she can forget that her husband still needs sex to keep his procreative ability healthy. (A study in the 1970s discovered that some men who had sex less than once a month had a higher incidence of prostate cancer, but cancer happens in the best of marriages. Google, Web MD- Health and sex.) The Bible exhorts us to yield to each other in a marital way. It is observable that the kind of work the man does can influence how often he feels the need for comfort from his wife. A deep love inspires reverence and gentleness. Animals wait until the female shows she is ready—something that some men could take notice of. She doesn't have to be grabbed; if she loves you, she's not going away soon.

It has been observed that a man can need a woman more often than a woman needs a man, but some women are just as hungry for male attention as men are. A story was told of a mature couple who had an active sex life, and she was healthy and happy until he had a heart attack. Without sex for a time she, became arthritic and bedridden until he became well enough to resume marital relations. This kind of dependency emphasizes the fact that we need each other physically, emotionally and spiritually, because love is in our spiritual realm and is the glue that makes everything good and worthwhile to the human race.

God, as the author of it all, knows our every strength and weakness. He knows the reason I am here when I ask Him for forgiveness, and I feel that He is very near.

Some people (especially guys) fall in love once and mate for life; other ladies don't seem to attract them anymore. They only have eyes for their wives; the wives are their inspiration, their reason for living. They are lighthearted and feel as if they can conquer the world. If the wife dies or rejects him, he can feel it like a death, It is the death of that first precious hope, and though through a good conscience, he can go on and marry after having lost so severely once. His ability to be that optimistic again can be severely limited, and though he can remain true to a future love, he may feel a compulsion to go on looking; which is not very pleasing to his new mate. (I know this from personal experience.) With her surplus of emotional capacity, she can move on more easily than he can, and she often does in today's society. She has inherited a tenacity for life from her forbears, they, having survived the loss of a mate many times in past centuries. A man leaves no such ability to his sons by dying, but the counsellors I've either read or spoken to haven't mentioned it, which is not very helpful. This was noted especially by divorcees in the single-parent club's discussion group—the very sensitive problems that could cause life-long hang-ups were left to the psychiatrists to divulge, most often taking them away from godliness. This poem relates something of what I learned.

The Way We Are (Left, Bereft or Divorced)

We've been hurt so badly, we may want
love but not marriage again.
Some of us find out (sadly) when a heart
breaks, it hurts just the same.
It wasn't the fact it was legal; that
makes us feel rejected and hurt.
It is because pride and love are integral.
We feel neglected and dragged in the dirt.
Man in his natural nature, for his self
has the greatest respect;
Anything that makes him feel guilty, he
is inclined to despise or reject.
If offered the heart of another—obviously quite a prize—
Unless he can feel he is worthy, he
is apt to reject or despise.
This may be why many won't accept God or saviour,
But remain tied down to their sins.
It's so hard to change our behaviour,
to feel we are worthy of Him.
God, knowing we're weak, made it easy
by prepaying it all on His cross.
Even though our stomachs feel queasy, when
we wonder how much it will cost,
We simply need to stand up and be counted,
then kneel in repentance to Him.
He'll take the weight from our shoulders;
with faith, peace enters in.
If we can learn to think more kindly,
we are better off by far,

For we become the way we think, we
tend to think the way we are.
But if the wrong path is taken, we can
find ourselves in deep grief
And feel that we've been forsaken by our own unbelief.

If I have the opportunity when talking to people, I like to tell them that human lives go through growing cycles like plants. In our spring time of romance, our flower bush comes out in bloom and we're ecstatic, but gradually the flowers fade and fall off, and all there is left is the green leaves. As the fall and winter of our lives come on, even those leaves wither and fall off, and all that we can see are the branches. In a marriage this is when some people get out their axe and even dig up the roots, even though the roots still show life. If we can have faith that they will grow again, it can come into bloom in the next spring time of our lives, but if we insist on finalizing the destruction of even the roots, (lawyers tend to do that), then the hole in both lives will stay to haunt them, making it even more difficult for them to make and keep future promises. Some divorced women in our club pretended to be widows, because men had trouble believing that they could hold her interest when another pretty good man had failed. Some men in single parents shunned them, and for good reason: at least two of our widowed men who took a chance with divorcees were divorced again within a year if they had children. Either that; or they lost their children, who had to live somewhere else. I had inside knowledge, having been a facilitator of our discussion group; it was usually a woman who phoned me in the evening, because my number was on our bulletin.

Calls could last from a half hour to three hours. I learned that when my own psychiatrist treated me for depression, a half hour was required to simply to break the ice each time.

This is another example of putting the stress on feelings instead of duty. The man who started The Salvation Army, weak and penniless, sent a telegram to a special meeting of executives with one word on it: "Others." Christ showed us the way to do it.

When Love Walks In

When love walks in, the dark clouds fly away.
When love walks in, we're in for happy days.
Keep love down in your heart, a smile upon your face;
Joy then becomes a part of each and every place.
Hope like a flame burns bright, dispelling clouds of gloom
When casting loving light into our living room.
God is on our side, making bright the way.
Happy as a bride, we look forward to each day.
A spring is in your step, a lilt is in your voice
When this person you have met becomes the final choice.
The loneliness departs to a remote place unknown,
And now two joyous hearts can share a happy home.
Let some joy overflow to those who know despair,
So everywhere you go, love will be in the air.
A gentle word, a friendly act, and heaven is on your side.
New hope becomes a fact to those hurt deep inside.
For love can fill the place where emptiness remained,
A smile can wreath a face where once was mirrored pain,
And you can play a part in God's almighty plan

Through an understanding heart and willing hands.
Why should despair remain and teardrops dim their eyes
When God can ease their pain
through help from you and I?
Joy can fill a heart up to its very brim'
Fear and despair depart when love walks in.
What is love but care? What is joy but hope?
To know someone is there can give us strength to cope.
Faith is an inner thing, born of courage to trust'
When we have it. our hearts sing down deep inside of us.
Exultation comes from faith. a knowledge of real worth.
When we have found our place, our niche upon this earth,
To strike a humble pose to the world may seem quite odd,
But our minds know sweet repose
and the strength that comes from God.

White Owl

High on a hill top, a fox is barking at the moon,
While off in the distance, he hears the laughter of a loon.
Moonlight dances on the water while
wavelets hiss upon the shore,
A never-ending sequence that goes on forever more.
He tells stories around the campfire
while his papoose lies asleep,
Or joins the others singing to the
tom-tom's rhythmic beat.
He relates what his grandfather told
him, of Mother Earth so long ago,
Before he took his final walk into a drift of snow;

Donald Dolson

Of how a flock of pigeons could block out the noonday sun,
And the air is filled with thunder
when the buffalo would run;
How the fish were clean and plentiful,
and everything seemed good.
But now the water's dirty, there's no refuge in the woods.
For now some trees are dying from
the pollution in the air,
And the sound of chainsaws can be
heard most everywhere.
He sees how white man's progress
brings so many so much pain,
And he wonders if it's nearly time for good to come again.
He stares at the campfire as though into eternity,
nd he sees more in the embers than there's ever on TV.

Some years ago in Toronto, I was a member of (Canadians Allied in Solidarity with Native People (CASNIP) until the office had insufficient funds to continue. My respect is still with them. Some of my ancestors, having arrived 200 years ago, have been linked with native people, although we have traced our own beginnings back to Dalfsen, a village in Holland in the 1600s.

AD 2400

I'm one of the people who lived long ago,
in a world of great splendor, of power and show.
We had aeroplanes, rocket ships, automobiles,
all manner of things on floats, skids or wheels.

We got tired waiting on nature with
her timeless treasure.
We wanted everything quick and at hand for our pleasure.
Our power-making machines put
smoke and fumes in the air,
Which killed plants birds and bees,
and people died in despair.
But we had to go on so we could make a buck.
If you got left behind, you were just out of luck.
The waste from our homes, our factories and farms,
Put filth in the water and caused much alarm.
We put poison in the water so no bad microbes could live,
But we lost the benefits the good ones could give.
We poisoned the insects, too numerous for words,
And this ended up by killing most birds.
We remembered too late we had to
be young to have young.
We were too intent on pleasure and having our fun.
Our air and water had to be filtered
to breathe or to drink;
Everywhere we went, we had both dust and stink.
We didn't leave room for children,
for playgrounds or parks.
We became a society without soul or heart.
Everyone wanted to get, no one wanted to give;
It eventually became too expensive to live.
No one cared for the buildings;
Balconies tumbled down;
Some people found it a long way to the ground.
Though politically corrupt, we were still very proud;
No other opinions were ever allowed.

And so we suffered from internal decay,
And our civilization just wasted away.
While the true native peoples,
With bows, arrows and spears,
Took fish from the rivers and hunted the deer.
Their waste turned to plant food by natural means;
They didn't dilute and drink it
through expensive machines.
Our tall buildings decayed and turned into dust;
Our fancy bridges crumpled and turned into rust.
Where huge factories growled, they just take their ease
Amid the chirp of the birds and the buzz of the bees.
They learned to live with nature,
and appreciate her worth.
The "meek" did indeed inherit the Earth.

Chapter 4

The Basic Revelations in the Dolson Theory

Sir Isaac Newton became famous for his theory of gravity after seeing an apple falling from a tree. His idea was helpful, and he was a superb mathematician and provided many calculations still in use. But like Benjamin Franklin, who assumed that the battery pole he called positive had the surplus of electrons, it wasn't fully true. Newton's suction or attraction idea itself fails to answer how we can have volcanoes, which exhibit an extreme inner pressure. The theory of Franklin was proved wrong by the electron theory: it was actually the reverse, and the negative pole was the donor. However, electricity doesn't care what we call it and works either way. The NPN and PNP transistors are a good example.

The same appears to be true to some degree with gravity. How can we have a volcano, if gravity were to be a suction or attraction? When we ride in a vehicle or are flying on an aircraft, we can't tell whether we are being pulled from the front or pushed from the back, but the overall scheme demands more accuracy in space. Volcanoes act more like safety valves, letting off excessive pressure from the center of the earth from a build-up of heat, possibly from the decay of gravity waves from space. Their energy melts both lava and the iron core, which is assumed to facilitate our magnetic poles. The key as I see it is like a transmitter (by vibrating space, by moving electrons in a predetermined way) it can transfer information by sending the electron movements to an antennae, to be transmitted in order to be received, with its audio portion heard by a listener or seen on the video on a monitor.

Space moved by the motion of other heavenly bodies will have some effect on our Earth, at least in weather patterns. All of this comes from the fact that an electron acts opaque to space: move an electron, move space; move space, move an electron. It's all around us and in every created object, including us.

While studying air-conditioning, refrigeration, appliance repair and oil burner servicing at Standard Engineering in Toronto in the early 1960s. I was retraining after a debilitating home accident. I observed our teacher using an Amprobe (commercial name for a meter measuring current in an alternating current circuit). It indicated the number of amperes flowing by the intensity of the magnetic flux around each wire. (The probe arms encircled a single wire; if placed around both wires, the alternate phases would cancel and create a null reading.) I asked the teacher what the magnetic flux was made of, and he said it was an effect. I knew it was an effect, but what was it made of? He couldn't tell me, and neither could anyone else. I noticed while living on our farm that if I placed my finger in a full cup of water, it would overflow, but what is in a wire that is forced out when voltage puts electrons in? I had received my radio TV technician certificate at Radio Electronic Television Schools in Toronto in 1957, and I heard of the man who had looked into a copper wire with an electron microscope and observed that atoms were almost vacant space; it was like looking at a starry sky, with more space than solid objects. This suggested three things to me.

1. An electron is opaque to space. Like an ice cube in water, if you move the ice cube, you move water. If you move water, then you move the ice cube. The ice cube is water in a solid state. An electron appears to be a ball of compacted space, or Higgs-Bosons or God particles, which I think of as magnetons because magnetism appears to be a flow of space as illustrated by the Amprobe and the flux around the wire.

2. Space appears to be incompressible; it accurately responds to space movement from impulses centuries apart to trillions of impulses per second, as illustrated by light waves, with our eyes able to register the colour of objects in the 430–790 trillions of impulses per second. Ultraviolet is beyond our visual ability; the frequency is too high for our eyes to register.

3. Space behaves like a liquid under infinite pressure, and our whole solar system is carried along in a mammoth stream of space, travelling at hundreds of thousands of miles per hour through the Milky Way Galaxy. We feel as if we're standing still, but it is all relative.

To me, my Newton-like moment was like finding the Rosetta stone of electronics, opening the door to a completely new way of comprehending electrical effects. We appear to be in a sealed circuit, enclosed in this incompressible fluid like medium, under infinite pressure, which we call space. By looking at it as a superfine liquid, we ought to be able to measure its viscosity by its reaction time of 186,300 miles per second, the speed of light. One man years ago suggested that in effect, space was harder than the hardest steel. We see this proven every time we use our car door opener: the miniscule gigahertz signal goes through doors and windows, and we take it for granted without wondering how this feat is accomplished. If we look at everything as being part of a single unit, the reason for the effect in one area being transferred to the rest becomes obvious. There is no physical flow like wind; a space particle bumps the next one to it, like a freight train shunting, and the energy is transferred to the adjacent one. It may be in wood, glass, concrete or whatever. Bosons and electrons are closely linked and fully cooperate instantly to transfer the impulses.

Each impulse, regardless of its origin, contains a small part of the energy that created it, and like the waves on water following each other, they are additive in effect. In 1973, I was interviewed by Marq de Villiers for an article on the possibility of creating an all-permanent magnet motor. It was treated like fantasy, another searcher for perpetual motion, as if that were impossible, but in fact our world runs on it.

I learned years later that Howard Johnson of Blacksburg, Virginia, patented an all-magnetic motor in 1973. Patent

#4,151,431 Parts to make one can be found on your computer. It is possible but as yet impractical because the magnets and mechanical parts are expensive, and its output is low, even though free.

I coined the acronym FILIM to describe space as a Frictionless (or nearly so) Incompressible Liquid, Invisible Medium under infinite pressure. This is proven by the production of light, and explosions of gas clouds in space, the big explosions create new heavenly bodies. A piece from one such explosion went across Russia on February 18, 2013, and fragments broke thousands of windows while the main part of its body passed by. In 2010, Dr. Paul Corkum of the National Research Council in Ottawa, Canada, photographed an electron using a laser flash of one Ato second.1/000,000,000,000,000,000,000,000[th] of a second. Nature operates from the miniscule to the gigantic, and everything has a purpose for something, somewhere.

Without our magnetic poles, our Earth might have moved erratically as well; we needed something to stabilize our movements, and it does.

It was stated on the radio in 2011 that the energy from our sun comes in high-frequency, direct-current impulses. Like waves from dropping something in water, the rings move in one direction, however space completely surrounds the source; and the pattern can't help but be different.

Stars behave in like manner; the fact that we can see their light means that a portion of their energy is reaching us from all directions. Each impulse carries a minute part of the original force that created it, and I've wondered if the combined residual effects of countless waves enter our earth and have their decay create the heat to melt the lava in our core after providing us with gravity. Most people have seen how a magnifying glass can focus sunlight to a point and even burn paper. Lower frequency radio waves can also be focused; we see it in dish antennae where the wave energy is focused to obtain the strongest signal strength for TV reception.

With light being space pulsating in the optical segment of the electromagnetic spectrum of frequencies, and with a permanent magnet appearing to be an eddy current of space, I envision the possibility of using a permanent magnet to produce light at low cost with neither noise nor pollution. Permanent magnetism acts like a direct electrical current; to produce light, its movement would have to be interrupted at the frequency of light. Could that be accomplished by pressure on a piezoelectric crystal? The wind has been harnessed to create electricity; the constant effects in permanent magnets (possibly maintained by our movement through space) could be a wonderful help to people in isolated locations and with little money, if manufacturers would be altruistic for the sake of humanity. I remember when going to the moon was considered impossible, and now it's possible. It was contemplated by Mr. Goddard in the 1930s, and he got called "Moony Goddard." It was his patents printed in *Scientific American* literature that gave Von Braun the idea for rocket-propelled "buzz" bombs used in the Second World War.

The fact that a 10–20 watt transmitter on Mars can send a signal to be picked up on Earth indicates that the stars are feeding energy into the incompressible medium we call space, keeping it vibrating simultaneously at a host of different impulses per second, causing harmonics and heterodyning at a myriad of frequencies. I believe that this complex action gives us what we call weight and gravity, as I already suggested. With electrons being opaque to space movement, these impulses strike the electrons and atoms in our atmosphere and collectively inhibit space movement, creating pressure on our air, water, and the earth; we call it gravity. The inhibiting effect of the atoms and electrons in our air put 14.7 pounds per square inch on the Earth at sea level, and over 46,000 tons of air pressure on each acre of land. Water has many more electrons per square inch than air, so one yard high of a square inch of water has more resistance than the total air pressure, at 16.02 pounds per square inch of water. Add this to the air pressure, and you can see why volcanoes spurt high into the air. If my observations and calculations are right, it explains why oxygen levels on a mountain at 10,000 feet are higher than over land, and how there could be a variation depending on the height and volume of the mountain with its ability to inhibit slantwise gravity waves from the stars, which travel in straight lines, with the mountains being larger or smaller or shorter. Mass inhibits radiation of all kinds, from the resistance of the electrons to space movement, a primary source.

Without our air pressure we would have no water, because water turns to gas at zero pressure. Without green vegetation creating oxygen through photo synthesis, our earth would be as void of life as our moon is. Atmospheric pressure on a heavenly body seems to depend on the mass of the body and its ability to inhibit the movement of space waves vibrating energy all around it. God didn't forget anything, but we lose air to space while we go around on our orbit, and if we didn't continually create more oxygen from photosynthesis, nearly every living thing on our world would die.

It also seems to me that the depth and density of atmosphere on a heavenly body is determined by its mass, and so a small one won't hold enough atmospheres to nourish life as we know it. After about a ten year journey, the European Space Agency has landed its Rosetta satellite on a comet with little gravity, November, 2014. (if gravity is the reciprocal of mass they can gauge its mass by its strength of gravity.) Scientists discovered that our world has a tail we can't see, similar to a comet, and they have mapped out its shape and composition. They found it from seeing satellites falling to earth prematurely after they travelled through it.

A demonstration given to pilot trainees showed in a room imitating the conditions at ten thousand feet, with less oxygen, helping them to learn that normally people go to sleep from lack of oxygen at 10,000 feet. In parts of the world people live and work at 15,000 feet or more, and even though the air is thin, people unaccustomed can still stay awake. It was illustrated on a graph I saw years ago, showing an upward curve on mountains. Apparently the mountain mass has a shielding effect against slant wise gravity waves casing oxygen to cling at higher levels. Gravity waves seem to dissipate their energy by creating heat in the core of our world through their loss of energy, keeping the magma liquid.

When it takes trillions of electrons to create a grain of sand, some idea as to how tiny the building blocks of earth really are can be appreciated, and we don't know if what we call God particles are the tiniest. Spirits may be even tinier in a realm we know very little about, but many people refuse to admit that there are spirits or that any are needed, perhaps wanting to avoid any feeling of indebtedness to God, for what He made which includes everything, and that God is still here in His creation.

A fetal heartbeat begins at between 10–12 weeks after conception, when an electrical impulse coming from the sinus node of the tiny heart gives the signal to start its regular sequence of muscular contractions to force blood through its tiny body, for possibly a hundred years. Who but God could send that starting signal and keep it going? Each warm-blooded creature has an aura of both infrared (heat) and ultraviolet light that owls, cats, and some other creatures can see at night, but they can't see a dead body; it loses its aura when the spirit of life departs.

Animals, birds and even undersea creatures follow lines of force and instinctively keep in touch with others of their own species. Dogs, horses and cats have shown an out-of-this-world kind of knowing intelligence, not only of each other but of human beings as well, saving people's lives. These special waves can be disrupted by our transmitters; on a lake near what was our dew line (distant early warning). Up north in Canada, the operators noticed one autumn that a large flock of geese on the lake were very agitated, and the geese stayed there even though it was time to migrate. One person wondered if it was due to their transmitter, so they turned it off, and the geese immediately flew off now that the signal they needed was available. Distance seems to have no effect on prayers; they seem to follow the same impulses used in nature.

I studied radiation monitoring while a volunteer member of North Metro Emergency Measures (Toronto) during the atomic scare in 1959; it was called "Eleven Steps to Survival." I also learned basic rescue, radio telephone operating, NATO alphabet, and St. John's Ambulance first aid, plus radiation monitoring for people working with radioactivity or in a disaster area.

A dosimeter for people dealing with radioactive situations was worn like a wrist watch, and the indicating hand was made of quartz fiber with a negative charge. Material in the operators blood had become radioactive radiateing God's particles (space). The radiation steals electrons from the needle, allowing it to fall back, which gives an indication of the amount of the radiation received by the wearer. A level of 10 milliroentgen is not considered dangerous on each person; our bodies can replace blood cells fast enough to compensate. However, it can be additive: if 10 people were to be close together with that amount on each one, they would each receive 100 milliroentgen, which would be another matter.

Intense radiation kills the corpuscles in our blood. A similar effect can be seen on street lights, where their illuminations overlap: the light is brighter where they touch, but that is without any danger. I suggest that atoms are sped up by radioactivity, and that space particles fly off like sparks from a grinding wheel, turning electrons back into space. The particles flying off from centrifugal force are replaced in the atom from a flow called centripetal action. In what seems to be a sealed circuit, every action creates a reaction; when space actually flows in any direction, it has to be instantly replaced by more space.

A permanent magnet may be an illustration of what is happening at the atomic level of each atom at a lesser speed. (We are in a closed circuit.) A similar effect can be noticed when a laser instrument is used to drill holes, cut metal or do surgery: there appears to be a lack of residue, suggesting that the electrons in the material removed have been dismantled and turned back into space material.

What scientists have been calling dark matter" appears to me to be the basic space material that God used to make everything. I think of it as the amniotic fluid of the universe because everything has been created in it and of it. Scientists do an autopsy" to see God's handiwork.

Nature has a habit of repeating the same steps in different situations. On our farm I often saw dust devils" (little whirl winds) toss dust in the air for a few seconds, much bigger whirl winds crossing a hay field tossed the hay from hay-cocks high in the air along a path we would have to re rake it to get our hay back. I also noticed while watching a small stream, how little eddy currents changed constantly as they were swept downstream even though the stream bed stayed the same, new ones took their place. Vortexes in a river have occasionally picked up stones from the bottom and deposited them on top of the ice from the momentum of the stream. Ice is thinner where water swirls, and so it may have been ejected when there was a bit of open water; it later freezes, and a stone appears from nowhere.

With space acting like a fluid, I picture black holes as vortexes of space in space.

In August 2011, scientists watched a black hole dismantle a star, like a buzz saw going through wood. The intensely moving space took its atoms apart. Everything is made from space, and so this is natural because when space moves, it moves electrons. It is easy for electrons to move space; our power transformers are dependent on this action, and electrons under voltage pressure push space in and through secondary windings, causing electron flow according to the size of the wire and the number of turns compared to the number of those in the primary. Voltage also follows in like manner, with the number of watts being related to the intensity of the magnetic field, and this is dependent on the amperage of the flow. An iron core facilitates the action; an air core is much less effective. Material drawn into a black hole is dismantled bit by bit; its high–speed, circular movement is obvious, and though a black hole looks very shallow from the Hubble telescope, it could be many thousands of miles thick because of the immensity of our universe. Light is space pulsating in the optical range of the electromagnetic spectrum, and so light would also disappear in a black hole when the portion of space vibrating in that range is sucked in.

Black holes appear to be the garbage rooms of space. If material was instantly converted to its original material, it wouldn't appear black, so they look like staging areas, perhaps clouds of atoms. Scientists will undoubtedly find out, or at least try.

The truly miraculous way everything works together should prove to those who really want to know that we do have a great God. He is greater than we can imagine with our finite minds, and we can exist only as long as His power keeps our sun and stars providing the constant electronic vibrations that keep the electrons and atoms spinning.

God is a powerful spiritual entity necessary for our continued existence, and He will continue to offer His directions for a long, happy, healthy, guilt-free life if we will accept His love and follow His rules. The Ten Commandments were given for our benefit as our guide to achieve a long, happy, guilt-free life; they are operating instructions and guard rails for humans along the road of life.

People constantly wonder how God can stay out of tragedies when we are told how He watches over us. When my first wife died from being struck by a car, I wondered, too, until it came to me that if God stopped us from being cruel and inconsiderate in any number of ways, He would be denying someone his or her free will. He promised us our free will, and He can't be untrue to Himself, He won't lie. With God being the giver of our life spirits and the keeper when we return to Him, what we look upon as tragedies may, to Him, be simply a teaching experiences. He is able to salvage good from anything that happens: "I will repay," saith the Lord.

If we will look around carefully, we can see that God is definitely pro-creation. Everywhere we look, we see various forms of life, each going through its own special sequence. When the environment becomes difficult, all forms of life are forced to try to adapt; this stress causes animals and people, as well as vegetation, to become more conscious of the need to procreate their own species. We see plants that can grow a foot or more if in good soil, but when growing from a crack in the pavement, it may come into bloom when small in size, in the hope of making seeds to extend its kind. People under stress tend to become more sexually conscious, especially noticed in our armed forces.

The possibility of not living long is a constant thought in the back of their minds, and they hope to receive the satisfaction and excitement that comes from planting their seeds. Few people seem to understand that the feeling of joy and lightheartedness, just in anticipation, comes from the possibility of being involved with the bringing of a new life to enjoy all the beauties that the earth provides. The culmination of this hope, all the pleasurable feelings are stored in the subconscious mind, becoming the power of suggestion.

We respond to a system of rewards, and being included in a part of God's creation becomes indelibly fixed in our memory. First impressions are often the deepest, with everything that happens later being unconsciously compared over even a lifetime.

Our Judeo Christian Bible states, "As a man thinks, so is he." A thought precedes each of our actions, and with God's advice and help we can steer our actions in the most helpful direction. The success we achieve is shown by our actions: "by our fruits we are known." Because of Satanic forces, some people seem unwilling to believe that all God's laws were designed to give us our best possible way of living, with the least hurt for all and our greatest satisfaction.

Actions speak louder than words, and God's actions prove the great love He has for each of the human beings He created. He is also impartial: rain falls on the just and the unjust. It shows in many ways and gives us ample opportunities to ask His forgiveness for being disobedient of His commands. His first edict for anyone breaking any one of His Ten Commandments was death. A close observation could show that this could be a literal observation, because failing to follow any one of the last eight commandments could get one killed by violence or disease over time. Like any loving father, He wants what is best for the children He created. His first accommodation for failure to follow His instructions, or simply being disobedient, was to demand something of value to be brought to the synagogue and have it killed by a rabbi. It could be an unblemished calf, lamb or dove according to the person's means. To make us aware that He meant what He said, He arranged it so it would be costly for us to be disobedient; this proved inadequate, and so to prove He knew all the ways we feel, He sent a portion of His spirit to create His son by way of the womb of a young virgin Jew impregnated by His Holy Spirit. Jesus would go through all the phases people experience. Jesus not only fulfilled the Ten Commandments, but He became the perfect sacrifice to pay for all our disobediences past, present and future.

This did not give us freedom to disobey at will, but it gave God the opportunity to reclaim those who in their hearts were genuinely sorry for how they broke His laws. This is love in its divine form, free to honest believers. He is still waiting for the surrender of more of His created beings. God and His heavenly host are joyful when even one sinner repents his past rebellious deeds and vows to keep on the path He has designated. His love includes people of every colour, race and creed.

Some native tribes and other people with little or no formal education have found their way to God by knowing little more than John 3:16–17. God didn't send Jesus to condemn anyone, but through belief in Jesus they could be saved from their dismal, hopeless lives. Now they belong and can feel accepted by the greatest love ever shown! I don't call it a story, because it's an absolute fact seen all around us.

God shows His love in every living thing: each infant, flower, grass, tree, animals, bird—the list is endless, and unless God remains present, nothing we see could stay here, because it requires some kind of force to be applied constantly to keep atoms and electrons continually rotating to maintain each and every object, and a spirit to direct and motivate the actions. The complexity, intricacy and time sequencing is mindboggling.

Few people have connected geologic findings to the immense effort God made to create the world we now enjoy and to make it habitable, such as the collisions of other heavenly bodies that gave us our moon, born from a portion of our original sphere and rounded by magnetic effects pulling equally in all directions. It appears that the original parent of our Earth was a huge ball of hydrogen and oxygen gas, which became our oceans through God's will. The early Earth had immense forests and huge reptiles.

Over the millennia, a huge event caused the Earth to be stirred like a pail of mud; forests and animals were buried deeply in the Earth, creating seams of coal from the vegetation being compressed deeply in the earth. This also gives us our gas and oil. My parents, on a trip to Pennsylvania, brought home a piece of anthracite coal with the imprint of a leaf clearly etched in its surface, clearly indicating from where it came.

Our sun appears to rotate the Earth by hitting it on the side, like the skin effect of a bladeless turbine. If a blast of cosmic energy were to hit our earth on a slant opposite to its direction of rotation and slow down the surface of our world, the momentum of the inner portion could push tectonic plates under one another, causing mountains to rise. The immense weight of water would assist the moving of earth and rocks, as is seen in so many flooded areas. The direction of each mountain chain would indicate the way the world was turning at that time, and if the age of each chain could be measured accurately, the sequence of time between episodes could be estimated.

Geologists have seen proof of earlier disasters from excavations and land formations; huge fissures in the ocean bed could indicate from where much of the material for the mountains came (e.g., the Marianna Trench). Seismic tests have shown that the Earth's crust is deeper under mountains, perhaps showing where a portion of a tectonic plate is residing. When tectonic plates were first envisioned, they were disputed until the undersea movement caused a transatlantic cable to be pulled apart; continental drift was established as a fact from that episode. It also tells us how snail shells and remnants of undersea creatures are found on the tops and sides of mountains, far from the bodies of water seen today.

The resistance electrons present to the movement of space causes objects to be pushed to other objects from their shielding effect on each other. This is plainly illustrated in the formation of the tides on our earth, and the most obvious is that created from moon shadow. It shields the earth as it circles us, creating a difference in potential that causes the water to rise from being pressured by the gravity waves from space. Even though the sun is much further away, it is also much larger, and so it affects the movement of oceans as well. When the sun and moon are diametrically opposite, we can have a tide effect showing on both sides of our world simultaneously. The tide differentials are constantly changing but are uniformly predictable because they go through the same rotations on a regular basis, with differences of intensity at times.

All of God's creations work together in some mysterious ways at times. With our sun so close, why doesn't our weight vary from night to day? Can it be that these other much larger heavenly bodies have so much more effect on us that the sun's effect is miniscule in comparison? It appears to me that there are more facets of power influencing our earth and everything else around it than we have realized.

Our Earth has been relatively stable over many years, but we live in constant danger of objects traveling at very high speeds and running into us, as has happened in the distant past, and so each day is actually very precious to us. I hope the information and ideas I have expressed point out our need to more closely follow what God has designed and planned for us in His word.

If we could all realize how dependent we are on each other for our own well-being, we could expect that world peace would occur. Many are waiting for Christ to come again and make this accomplishment a reality; it is our heartfelt hope because our world deserves appreciation, and Christ is the one to make sure we get it. We can play a part if we are obedient.

Summary of the Dolson Theory
(An abbreviated version, much more has been written)

The GEMS of God's creation—Gravity, Electricity, Magnetism and Space.

Space—God's raw material, a frictionless, incompressible, liquid, invisible medium, or FILIM. It encompasses everything and is an integral part of all creation, composed of infinitely tiny parts, perhaps thousands compressed in one electron.

Electron—A tiny sphere, opaque to the movement of space: move space, move an electron; move an electron, move space. In solid form, an electron appears to be compacted space. Dr. Paul Corkum of the National Research Council, Ottawa, photographed an electron in 2010 using an Ato second laser burst. I met him when he spoke at RCI in Toronto in 2010, and I told him some of my ideas.

Atom—A congregation of electrons and assorted complimentary parts, with a host of combinations producing all the visible objects we can see, spinning rapidly, having gyroscopic action, centrifugal force and centripetal action. Their combined effect gives us inertia and momentum.

Gravity—The result of a combined contribution from the emanations of all the stars in our universe creating an endless number of direct–current, electromagnetic impulses (possibly focused by adjoining beams from stars in all directions) in this incompressible medium we call space, with harmonics and heterodyning, penetrating to the core of heavenly bodies.

Weight—The amount of resistance to space movement, which is determined by the number of electrons contained in the object resisting space flow.

Black Hole—A vortex of space in space, collecting space debris or planets, just as whirlpools in oceans collect floating objects. On August 25, 2011, scientists watched a black hole dismantle a star. This is to be expected because when space moves, it moves electrons, or star material.

Dark Matter—Unoccupied space. If it were dark in the ordinary sense, we wouldn't be able to see the awesome distances shown by the Hubble telescope.

Light—Space vibrating in the optical region of the electromagnetic spectrum of frequencies. With light being space, it automatically has the ability to move electrons. When it is accelerated, as in a laser (Light Amplification by Stimulated Emitted Radiation), light used in this way appears to be able to disintegrate atoms and electrons back into particles of space.

Radiation—Accelerated space particles accomplished by a speed-up of the movement of atoms and electrons past their normal speed, flying off like sparks from a grinding wheel. Big atoms coast (radiate) longer than smaller ones. This effect is illustrated in a dosimeter (an instrument worn on a wrist to tell the amount of radiation absorbed by a worker).

Magnetism—An even more mysterious phenomenon than the electron. It appears in a permanent magnet as an eddy current of space, with the steady characteristics of a direct current. It acts as though affected by capillary action, being observed in a number of formations, mostly iron, alnico magnets, aluminum lickel and cobalt, an Alnico magnet, used instead of field coils in loud speakers, as well as electric motors, plastic magnets, fridge door seals and more. The same space material acts like a pulsating direct current when used as gravity, and emanations from high-powered stars keep our incompressible medium in a constant state of high-frequency vibratory motion. Could it be what keeps our atoms and electrons constantly moving?

Gyroscopic Action—Spinning objects appear to defy gravity to some extent by their movement. In a gyroscopic compass, its tendency to remember its static position makes it possible for us to determine the direction we are going. Large gyros on aircraft carriers steady the deck to help planes take off and land, so the effect works both horizontally and vertically. Gravity waves come from all directions except from the Earth. Earth's mass is a shield, and the collective gyroscopic effect of spinning atoms and electrons could create what we call inertia and what we see as solid objects. Gravity waves seem to be thrown off by a spinning object.

A rapid movement of space, flowing like a liquid, is apparently able to separate solid objects and allow the atoms to reach their optimum position, as in magnetic forming, creating flared ends on hydraulic tubing for aircraft in Malton, Ontario. When atoms are accelerated even more, a solid object can become a cloud of innate particles, as shown in the speeding up of an electron to near the speed of light in a cyclotron years ago, when the electron was seen to bloom, suggesting it was made up of many space particles and confirming Albert Einstein's theory that it limited our speed of travel. Recent studies suggest that neutrinos travel faster than light, but they don't seem to construct material, and so Einstein is still right.

As with almost any theory, mine is incomplete with many flaws to be ironed out. It's simply an idea. Albert Einstein maintained that a good imagination is better than facts, because most people can learn to remember what has already been made, but imagination creates new ideas for inventions—a whole new world of objects and activities. I have suggested that permanent magnetism appeared to me to be a flow of space following something like capillary action in suitable materials, but space seems to be more complicated than that, possibly composed of more than one substance, just as atoms have numerous combinations.

We know that spinning objects can have gyroscopic action and that electrons are spinning in two ways simultaneously. With trillions of electrons in a grain of sand, is the ability to remain in one place due to the collective gyroscopic effect of all those spinning electrons? It seems possible to me; the area around us is vibrating with countless frequencies from the sun and stars, because space is incompressible. A small transmitter on Mars sends information millions of miles to Earth, and we see stars with much greater power.

If we ever get close to analyzing the Earth and environment by "autopsying" it, we will approach the spiritual realm, which is even more mysterious than our conscious area of seeing, touching and reasoning. Without spirits there would be nothing living, animate or otherwise; growing cells require some kind of direction to make a final product and remain here.

Canadian natives thought that all living things were spiritually related, and when the DNA molecule was analyzed, scientists discovered that in a way the natives were right every living thing be it animal, vegetable or human, every one is composed of various combinations of DNA.

Our sun striking our earth on an oblique angle could be causing our rotation, and with the Earth being composed of many liquid materials, a sudden gust of space wind from the opposite direction of our earth's rotation could cause a slowing in our surface. If strong enough, it could make mountains to rise from a tectonic plate subducting (going under an adjacent plate). The plate depth is thicker under mountains, and deep rifts like the Marianna Trench can be found in the ocean. Perhaps they were caused by the inner Earth momentum, and the angle of a mountain range formation could indicate the way the planet was turning at the time. A huge wall of water would assist earth movement, and measuring the age of each range could indicate the time lapse between occurrences.

Dr. Paul LaViolette (astronomer) stated that he thought a gust of cosmic rays caused decimation of life on Earth between 10–12 thousand year intervals, and we're nearly there. He also suggested a lesser one could have triggered the Asian tsunami. The water had seemed troubled (like blowing in a glass of water); with downward pressure, a plate could subduct under an adjacent one, raising the ocean like a blanket, pulling water away from the shore and increasing air pressure on animals ears (they fled for higher ground). Fish, swimming against the current when the ocean pulled back landed on the beach. The water moved back and forth until the energy was dissipated. It's a thought. Most of us fail to see how vulnerable our Earth is.

No matter what ray or type of radiation we encounter, they are all bits of space in some configuration, because space is the only raw material at the heart of everything. Apparently there are shafts of power flowing through space, acting like the blast of a jet engine. According to Dr. Paul LaViolette, there is a certain area in a part of space sending out these blasts of cosmic rays on a regular basis. We don't know what effect it may be having on other parts of the universe, and we may not be the only one being hit on a sequential basis of 10-12 thousand years apart, if his calculations are correct.

I am grateful to the scientists who have done so much for all humanity in all our fields of endeavour, but there is much that is left to do. The ideas I have expressed could fuel speculation for centuries—if we don't destroy ourselves first. At present we seem to be like children playing with matches, seeing how powerful atomic power is and how the radiation, once started, can't be shut off but will continue for thousands of years. We do not fully realize our need to treat it with more respect

The latest update.

The latest activity that tends to confirm at least part of my theory was in a science program on Television, in late September, 2014-10-05, put out by Natioal Geographic society concerning our Sun from The Goddard Space center. The announcer stated that the Sun depended opon "push gravity". It hasn't been widely accepted yet, if it ever will be, old ideas die hard, thinking of us living in a liquid like environment is difficult enough for most people.

I took another look at Nikolas Tesla's accomplishments: he has patented a way to get power from space in the U.S.A. (Google Nikola Tesla free energy,). it makes no atomic radiation, or pollution. It oprates on high voltage, but low amperage; it is complex.

#1 My assumptions: Star waves coming from all angles create a thrust that holds satellites in space, once they reach sufficient height above the earth for them to be struck from opposite sides past the earth.

#2 With the total volume of space being kept in a state of multiple high frequency from the emanations of countless stars, when their energy is impeded by another heavenly object, (The Sun or Moon) an area of lesser space pressure exists between it and our earth causing tides to follow the moon's shadow as well as that of the sun, water being a fluid.

#3 Cosmic waves hitting our earth can create tsunami's, or even mountain ranges if they are sufficiently strong, and arrive on the earth's side opposite to its present rotation, by holding back the crust, while the momentum of the core pushes tectonic plates under each other, creating mountains as the huge wave of water adds to the carnage. Angle of each range would indicate which way the world was spinning at that time

A Selection of Poems by Donald W. Dolson

An Operetta: "Love Song"

Just when I ought to be glad, why do I feel so blue?

Why, oh why, do I feel so sad, when I'm in love with you?
I wonder what you think of each day,
what do you dream of at night.
Will a small wedding be considered okay?
Will everything turn out all right?
Walking along with a lump in my throat,
silly old tears in my eyes.
Can't seem to laugh at the funniest joke,
don't know the reason why.
Then I see you come to the door. I
seem to go all weak inside.
My heart starts to thump even more than before,
And my chest is just bursting with pride.
Honey, gee, I love you so. It's awfully hard just to wait,

But I think the both of us know we
mustn't spoil our special date.

They Get Married

Longing, yearning to have you near,
Snuggled close in my arms.
I pray to God to protect you, my dear,
And keep you safe from all harm.
When I see that glow in your eyes,
The soft, melted look on your face,
My dear precious darling, I realize
Love like ours can't be bought at any place.

Together

Thank you, dear Lord, for sending
to us love so beautiful, free.
From the beginning You planned it thus,
To last eternally. Please help us to follow Your way;
Keep our love tender and warm,
careful in all that we do or say,
Saving our marriage from harm,
Living together in Your bosom of love, filled with humility,
Living our lives as designed from above
ever our eyes upon Thee.
Until at last, when our race is run,
And we're called to Your judgment throne,
May we hear You say, "My children, well done!
Welcome now to My home."

Lovers

When we see two lovers walking, it can make us realize
There are other ways of talking than to simply verbalize.
There's a gentle kind of shyness in
the way he holds her hand,
And our eyes might lose some dryness
if we really understand.
There's so much tender meaning in
the warmth of their embrace;
When their eyes are softly gleaming,
they seem lost in time and space.
If we could only capture the joy that's in a kiss,
We would have a spell of rapture—
but what price is there on bliss?
We can't put a price upon it, though the story's very old,
And we've read so many sonnets on a love as dear as gold.
Can they keep this joy in living as they
go on through their years?
They can if they keep giving, through their
smiles and through their tears.
They have to keep believing there's
some good in most of us,
And so go on investing by giving of their trust.

Love

Love gives us a reason for living;
love is long suffering, kind.
Love gives us the strength to keep giving,
to get peace and joy in our minds.
Love gives us hope for tomorrow;
love helps us to feel glad.
Love can ease all our sorrows so that we need not be sad.
Love is the source of our courage;
love is the light on our road.
Love can create a new age with man at peace in his abode.
Love can forgive the transgressions;
love can forget the deep hurt.
Love can make a confession and may
find a way that will work.
Love is the key to salvation; love is a power divine.
Love is the source of creation, love is of heaven's design.

Eyes of Love

Dad paid Mother a compliment, but
for why, she couldn't see.
"How could anyone feel romantic over
a dried-up old prune like me?"
The tired eyes, the greying hair would
hardly make him swoon.
The figure he saw standing there
might imply some other tune.
But he looks at her through eyes of love,
Through a gaze that's warm and tender.
His bride is who he's thinking of, so
that's how he remembers.
I've heard it said, I believe it's true:
that love is really blind,
And I think God made us that way to help us to be kind.

The Sun

With or without warning, each and every
morning, up climbs the sun.
Even if we cannot see it, we can surely
guarantee it: a new day has begun.

In all our lives there falls some rain;
We each receive a share of pain
Out of the blue.
But if we have faith, the sun is shining;
Behind each clouds, a silver lining.
We will pull through.

Up there above the clouds, a vale of sorrow's not allowed,
Just warmth and light.
There isn't any reason for days or even seasons
Beyond our sight.

If we watch the rain go, we sometimes see a rainbow
In the sky.
It tells an age-old story of some of heaven's glory
Up on high.

If we look at the colours in it, we
could find there any minute
The pot of gold.
For a moment we might capture all
the beauty and the rapture
A heart can hold.

There beyond our sight, that wondrous ball of light,
Right from our birth,
Shines there for all to see throughout eternity:
God's gift to earth.

Heart Talk

Have you ever heard the story of
how we get singing words?
They can be the nicest music that a mortal ever heard.

For they come right from our feelings
in a place down in our heart.
We can tell from the rhythmic beating
how the nicest of them start.

For our hearts are like wee children,
and they gabble all the time.
When they feel warm and happy, they
can overflow with rhyme.

But when they're feeling downcast,
the words can all be stilted.
There's no glory joy or beauty; they're
like a flower that has wilted.

Do you know what your heart's saying?
Have you ever stopped to listen?
You might hear it while you're praying,
and your eyes begin to glisten.

When our heads hear our hearts talking
and can make its wishes known,
The result can be quite shocking, for
the thing is called a poem.

Like someone learning dancing, there's
not much rhythm at the start,
And not much hope of nice romancing
in a mutilated heart.
But if we ask God to mend the tatters so
that it can beat again as whole,
All that seems to really matter, is to have a happy soul
My heart's a little pixie that bubbles
o'er with song and rhyme;
If it finds a place it could belong, it's singing all the time.

A heart can talk so deeply it is felt but never heard,
But when it's beating happily, it uses singing words.

A Single Parent's Carol for Christmas

When we have so many problems,
And we feel alone and blue,
How many of us think of God
As a single parent, too?
How He has many erring children,
But how He loves us one and all.
If we ask Him for forgiveness,
He'll be glad to hear our call.
We've heard how the Star of Bethlehem
On that cold, clear night did shine.
Let's bring His love light back this Christmas,
And put the Christ in Christmastime.
The pomp and show of this world below
Tends to dull His heavenly shine,
But His humble followers know
Through an inner glow
Of His love at Christmastime.
How the lovingest of fathers
The greatest price had paid,
For when Christ was born
on Christmas morn,
The gift of life was made.
How He grew up like an orphan,
Rejected and reviled,
For He was made of flesh and blood,
God's only begotten child.
We've heard how the Star of Bethlehem,
On that cold clear night did shine.
Let's put the Christ back into Christmas,
And show His love light all the time.

Canada

Canada, dear Canada, a sanctum of the free.
Your mountains, valleys, lakes and plains
Stretch out from sea to sea.
A land that nourished native folk,
The Eskimos and Indians,
Spread out her multicoloured cloak
And adopted new Canadians.

Canada, dear Canada, a land of stirring sights:
Of waterfalls, of geese that call,
And dancing Northern Lights.
The sugar maple, lonesome pine,
The beaver, fleur de lis
Are emblems of a land designed
With room for you and me.

Canada, dear Canada, the best of any age.
The North, the South, the East, the West—
A precious heritage.
A land where brave and noble dwell
In peaceful harmony.
A story we are proud to tell,
A splendid history.

Canada, dear Canada, a land where toil is blessed,
People of all nations, colours, and creeds
Carved homes from wilderness.
Echoes ring from distant shores,
From heroes in battle slain;
Their souls cry out forever more—
We're proud to own Thy name.
Canada, dear Canada, you teach us how to give,
By yielding part of Thy dear self
To all who in Thee live.
Could I but learn humility,
Of Thy greatness be a part.
To live with all in dignity
Through the vastness of Thy heart.

Focus

Keep your eyes ever up, focused on the sky.
Wherever peace and beauty glows, there go I.
Ask not of life, "What will I get?" But
"How much can I give?"
Of self, of joy, of peace and hope, to all of those who live.
From God we get; to God we give. His love awaits us yet,
For all the souls who today live, if we do not forget.
He made us, loves us, cares and waits
till we acknowledge Him,
And then His pearly gates swing
wide to let His loved ones in.
Look ever upward day by day, and never stay downcast,
For God is all along our way and waits for us at last.
Always give Him what He's due— your
life, your love, your hope—
And He will always see you through
and give you strength to cope.
A love forever, courage, and joy are
gifts sent down by Him.
When we repent and accept His son He forgives our sins.

Lord, We Forgive

Lord, we forgive that we may be forgiven.
How else can we have your precious hope of heaven?
We have no righteousness, that we can call our own.
You're the only way to our heavenly home.

There is nothing in this world that
can keep our hearts aglow,
Cheer us when we're sad, always lift us when we're low.
But there is one above who came down here below
To give us eternal love so that we can have an inner glow.

Yea, Lord, yea, down upon our knees,
We pray, Lord, pray, to receive Your heart ease.
The words in our hearts may only be a groan,
But You hear and can let a poor sinner come home.

Salvation

(to the tune of "There's a Fountain Filled with Blood")

A wanton heart goes through this life,
Bringing grief and pain.
With Your healing love,
Please, God, reach down,
And make it whole again.
In the darkest night, Your wondrous light
Of love, shines pure and clear
And those of us who see Your light,
Have little cause for fear.
The contrite heart who in this life
Will call upon His Name,
Will find a Friend, who in the end,
Will bring it joy again.
So laugh and sing; glad news He brings.
Your victory is near.
The prince of love waits up above;
Salvation day is here.
Be not afraid; your sins were laid
On His dear, precious head.
He asks us to live for Him now,
For He died in our stead.

Thanksgiving

(tune of "Doxology")

We thank Thee, God, for sun and rain,
For fruits of trees, of grass and flowers,
For joy that grows through toil and pain,
For freedom in this land of ours.

The streams and lakes are filled by Thee;
The mountains echo with Your praise.
Your bounty spreads from sea to sea,
Through all the golden harvest days.

When Jesus takes His harvest home,
May we be there within His store,
When He will claim us as His own.
True love is ours forever more.

Fruits of the spirit, all divine,
Flow from the fountain of His love.
We know it is thanksgiving time
Each time we pray to God above.

For now we feel His peace and joy
Bathed in the fragrance of His love.
Each man or woman, girl or boy
Can thank our father up above.

He hears the petitions that we make;
His heart is touched by humble praise.
If we will ask "For Jesus's sake,"
He will be with us all our days.

Jesus: Friend of the Poor

A spring of crystal clearness
In a land all parched and dry;
A light out in the darkest,
Furthest reaches of the sky.
Hope for all the hopeless
He has promised is in store.
A new joyfulness in living
When we've learned to trust Him more.
Warmth in every fiber
Of a heart once empty, cold;
Gladness where the sadness
Used to multiply tenfold.
Forgiveness for the sinner,
Through the son He sent to save.
Jesus Christ has been the winner
In His battle o'er the grave.
Exploitation of the helpless
Has forever been outlawed
By the righteous, tender mercy
Of our everlasting God.
For the poor, the weak, the helpless
Have a powerful, loving friend.
Pillagers of man and nature
Meet their creator in the end.

Reason

Love is our reason for living.
Love is a power divine.
Love can make us forgiving.
Love is of heaven's design.

Poverty

Some folks talk of poverty as if it was a joke.
They have money or property,
Can't imagine "Stoney broke."
They've never known the feeling
To be lying late at night, too hungry to be sleeping,
But you can't afford a light.
In your heart you may be praying
For just a little more,
But morning could bring more heartache
Than you had the day before.
I've got no indoor plumbing,
Electric lights or telephone.
If I want to do some smoking,
I get the makings, roll my own.
I'm thankful for my pension,
Though it's all too quickly spent
When I stock up on my cat food,
Buy stove oil and pay the rent.
There's no one left to care about me,
And so nobody knows
That my poor old Tabby died a long, long time ago.
For my friend I have my Bible, its pages badly worn;
A few of them are missing, and a lot of them are torn.

But it gives me peace and comfort
To know God loves and cares
About all of His children who are living everywhere.
I read about the people who lived so long ago,
And I find so many of them are just like folks I know.
Much of the world does not respect
the riches I have inside—
My God, my independence, and a little bit of pride.

Happy People

Happy the people whose God is our Lord,
For they shall find comfort in His blessed word.
He is our refuge in life's many storms;
His is the knowledge that keeps our hearts warm.
Comforted and sustained for as long as we live,
To Him all our praises in thankfulness we give.

A Whisper

I hear a soft whisper on the breeze,
Voices that I heard so long ago.
They bring me messages that please,
Things my heart will always know.
Love is always pure and good
When we trust our God above,
When we do the things we should,
And it's others we think of.
When we obey the laws of God's own son,
Our union will never be outlawed.
Our hearts beat together just as one,
And our lives are sanctified by God.
God does not unite our flesh alone
But joins together kindred souls.
When we find and know we are His own,
Our lives can be completely whole.

It Doesn't Matter

It doesn't matter the country we come from,
The colour of skin or whatever our size.
If it's love, food or shelter, we all need some.
Our longing souls peer out of our eyes.
We were put here for some purpose by God;
With faith and love we can get through each day.
We can get weary as onward we plod,
But God will help us if we're humble and pray.
We can learn to help one another
If we ignore the colour of skin.
He made us all equal as brothers,
To help in the world we are in.
God, may we ever be thankful
That we can grow in Your grace,
And of the others be thoughtful
Until at last we see Your face.

Our Lord

(to the tune "Because He Lives")

Our Lord came down; we called Him Jesus.
He took our place, He bore our shame.
Now in heaven, He will receive us.
Saved by His grace, we own His name.
Dear heavenly father, king of glory,
Maker of all that was or is,
We thank You for the wondrous story
Of how You showed Your love through His.
You sent Him down as a human baby
To know temptation and feel our pain.
Then to assure us of salvation,
He lived, He died, He rose again.
Now He's waiting up in heaven,
The author and finisher of our faith,
For He performed all that He promised,
And now in heaven we have our place.

True Love

True love is a cleansing thing; it burns refuse away
So a heart can truly sing without debris of yesterday.
And so a love is now; that is how it wants to be.
It declares its solemn vow, now to eternity.
And we can have its joy through faith, the gift of trust,
The means that God employs to speak to all of us.
Accept His gracious love, the gift of sin forgiven
Sent to us from above, the blessed fruit of heaven.

Heart Rich

He has only the cot that he sleeps on;
His clothes are mended and worn.
His pride in self and things is gone;
No more property than when he was born.
But he gives thanks to his creator
For supplying his daily bread,
For the well-worn cot that he sleeps on,
For the roof he has over his head.
He is not respected by people in general,
Who say he's an ambitionless clod,
But he appreciates all things eternal
And is loved by both children and God.
He works just for what he is needing
And helps others whenever he can.
He is honest and does no cheating;
He has respect for both God and man.
In his own quiet way he is happy;
He has peace and contentment within.
He isn't worried he doesn't look snappy
And is rarely tempted to sin.
He spends his life in forbearing
And is as good as most humans can be.
The kind of clothes he is wearing,
Won't matter in eternity.
Perhaps if we were not so ambitious
(Which can be a polite word for greed),
We could stop competing so vicious
And find the love we so sorely need.

Truest Love

True love is like a river flowing onward to the sea
From the heart of God the giver,
who cares for all humanity.
We can see Him in the sunrise as it
slowly wakes the earth.
We can see Him in a baby's eyes after
a mother gives it birth.
We can hear Him in the treetops as the
wind sighs through the boughs.
His joy in giving never stops, and He's thinking of us now.
How can we show appreciation for
all He gives to you and me,
For His blood bought our salvation
when He died on Calvary?
Can we be kind to one another, just
as thoughtful as can be?
Jesus loves us all as brothers and
paid the price to set us free.

Lost Love

We walked through a meadow, the
grass long and unmowed,
And we sat and we talked where the still waters flowed.
A sprig of a lilac I playfully stuck in your hair.
I can still smell the fragrance as we sat talking there.
We sat and we pondered just what living means
As we watched our reflections in that cool, limpid stream.
But where are the dreams that we had long ago?
They seem to have vanished like last winter's snow.
And where are you, darling? My heart wonders still.
Gone like the echoes from far away hills.
When was the last time I held you in my arms,
And kissed your sweet lips, so soft and so warm?
I pray, precious darling, wherever you are,
That God in His mercy will keep you from harm.
My mind still wanders back to those days long ago,
To the places, the people, and so many dreams.
It isn't the best way to spend time, I know,
But at times I still wonder just what living means.

Dear Mom

Mothers can be quite funny.
They can love even a naughty kid.
They only have to look at me
To know you were one who did.
You'd pat my bum and comb my hair,
Make sure my socks were a matching pair.
Wash my ears, and wipe my nose;
Make sure I put on all clean clothes.
Then make my lunch, send me to school,
Hoping I could learn some rules.
When I grew some more, you stayed up late
To see me safe home from a date.
There's little more that I can say 'Cept, "I
love you, Mom," on Mother's Day.

The River Of Love

Love is like a river that begins and ends in God.
Everyone who sails on it can be salvaged by His blood.
The ship that we are carried on is
known by the name of Faith;
It is propelled by a breeze of happiness,
filling the sails of grace.
It takes us from the slough of
Despond, on to the city of Joy.
There is room for every man or
woman and every girl or boy.
Starting in our infant years, we can be guided all the way
If we will listen to His call and just trust and obey.
The fruits of the spirit of His love from
that all nourishing stream,
God stores in mansions up above,
more beautiful than dreams.
Where can we find this river, lost in a valley of despair?
A desert of broken hopes and dreams,
filled with an awful fear?
The river is flowing at our feet, if we will but look and see.
The place where we all have to look
is The Book on Calvary.
The episodes contained therein all happened long ago,
But the tales go on repeating in everyone we know.
When we read this book, we're apt
to see the story of our life,
All our hopes and dreams, our work
and cares amid a sea of strife.
"I seem so often weary, Lord, and don't know what to do,

Even though You've told me of Yourself,
and where I can go to.
But why is it repeated so by all the human race?"
It was included in the Grand Design;
we each can choose our place.
Like a wheel caught in a rut, I go along each day,
Propelled as though by unseen hands
who want to have their way.
Constantly pulling at my soul, they carry me along.
Without Your strength to buoy me up,
my heart can have no song.
The song is hope and happiness, leading to the city Joy.
The rut is man's old sinfulness that Satan oft employs.
"Fear not, fear not, oh troubled soul,
your spirit's in My care.
You only have to say the word, and I always will be there.
Wherever you may be, whatever challenge looms,
My river of love, faith, hope and joy
dispel the clouds of gloom.
You know the master of the ship; you know He is the way.
You know that love, faith, hope and
joy are made to last always."
Oh God, Your help in ages past gave
hope for years to come.
Will help us to know the die is cast,
that heaven is our home.
When Jesus died upon the cross, He cried out, "It is done."
From that moment the price was paid,
and all our sins were gone.
We see by faith, the river wide, which leads to the city Joy.

Christ volunteered to be our guide
while we were girls and boys.
But we often let go of His hand and stumble on our way.
We sample things we know are
banned and subject to decay.
In pain and sorrow we limp back
to find the love we've lost,
But it's been there all the time since Jesus paid the cost.
We must repent and call on Him, and do it without delay,
To find the peace and confidence
that can be ours each day.
If we humbly board the ship of faith,
and all our gifts employ,
We'll find that we've been saved by
grace and enter into Joy.

I Became

Through pain and sorrow I became
what I was meant to be,
And I was meant to be a child of His,
So when I called upon His name, so that I could see.
Through all your life, He said, "Remember this:
All that glitters is not gold or brass
that's burnished bright.
And all the wealth the world can hold
won't give you peace at night.
But if you will just call on Me, I'll give you perfect rest,
And then throughout eternity you'll be among the blest."
So give your impoverished self to
Him, and do it without delay.
You'll find His precious peace within,
which will last for all your days.
Now I thank God with every breath
for sending us His son;
His spotless life and selfless death
brought hope to everyone.

Try to remember in all that you do
That God is loving and watching and caring for you.

Happy People

Happy are the people whose God is our Lord,
For they shall find comfort in His blessed word.
He is our refuge in life's many storms;
His is the knowledge that keeps our hearts warm.
Comforted, sustained, for as long as we live,
To Him, all our praises in thankfulness we give.

Bee Happy!

(Chorus) A honey bee lit on a buttercup,
But she fell off when the cup tipped up.
Nectar dripped upon the ground
While she went flying round and round.

A young mosquito, in her prime,
Is searching for a place to dine.
A tiny snap, a happy slurp,
A froggy's tongue has gone to work.
(Chorus)
A little brown duck and a big white drake:
See what a happy pair they make.
She'll fly off down to the creek,
But she'll be back within the week.
(Chorus)
My old dog blinks a bleary eye
When he sees me passing by.
I stroke his head and pat his rump,
And hear his tail go thump, thump. thump.
(Chorus)
A young man sees a pretty girl,
thinks that he'll give her a whirl.
She decides they'll do the town,
And both of them go round and round.
(Chorus)

Space

Space! The amniotic fluid of the universe,
Encompassing everything that was or is,
Present even in this humble verse,
Giving credit to the one whose power it is,
A frictionless, incompressible, liquid, invisible medium,
Space permeates everything as deep as prayer,
And though our lives seem filled with tedium,
Like God's love it is present everywhere.
It embraces every atom and electron;
Like gyroscopes, they are ever spinning, free.
The basic elements of all creation,
They are essential parts of you and me.
An enigma to every thinking creature,
Without space nothing could exist.
When we use it and obey the laws of nature,
True love and peace are ours if we persist.
For magnetism holds it all together,
Due to the flowing power of space.
With little noise and no offensive odour,
We gently glide from place to place.

Oh Lord

Oh Lord! Thou precious, blessed Lamb
Who died to set us free,
Thou wert, thou art, ever shall be,
From now to eternity.
Who hung the Earth in empty space,
A story ages old.
When asked, You simply said, "I Am,"
While yet the stars were cold.
Man was given heart, soul and voice,
A divine legacy.
And with these gifts he got a choice:
To be or not to be.
God has given Christ the power/
If we do as we are told:
Accept His son. and joy is ours,
Though stars wane and grow cold.

Mercy

A work of love is never lost in Jesus,
Though tempest tossed. it returns tenfold again/
For He promised He will never leave us
To all of those who put their trust in Him.
For all who give will also obtain mercy,
Though waves of doubt assail our ship with strife.
We will prevail if we persist in charity,
For in giving, we receive the gift of life.
If we don't grow weary in the act of giving,
We will mount up as though on eagle's wings;
We run the race for Christ while we are living
And know the joy that yielding to Him brings.
A life that is spent within His service
Is never lost, but will return again.
Though at times we do get tired and nervous,
He'll be with us through our time of pain.
Tried and true, we run the race before us;
In the end we know we'll find a sweet release.
As a part of a heavenly throng we join the chorus
And know the joy of perfect inner peace.

Do You Know?

Do you know your lord and master,
So infinitely kind?
Does your household ring with laughter
From a joy that is sublime?
When your house with joy is humming,
Then heaven will be your goal.
You know someday He's coming
To claim His salvaged souls.
There is comfort just in knowing
That His power is so divine,
That His grains of love are flowing
Through all the sands of time.
Our world is like a pebble
in the hollow of His hand,
And though our size were trebled,
We'd hardly make a grain of sand.
Though we are so tiny within His universe,
Our eyes get wet and shiny at the story of His birth.

Brotherly Love

Pure love is a beautiful thing;
When love is true, our hearts have wings,
Warmth as from a summer sky,
Faith that lasts as years go by.
If we see a brother err
And with his thinking not concur,
We can tell him of our saviour's love,
Our only way to up above.
We can try to be gentle, patient, kind,
For down there deep within our minds,
No matter what the others do,
We know we've done some erring, too.
When we can admit we make mistakes,
We might save someone a heart that aches.
When we can ask forgiveness, too,
Bigness of heart is showing through.
If we can do these things with grace,
We'll find we're welcome any place.
A love rests easy in our mind
When we know we have the nicest kind.

Happy Face

When I was young and barefoot, I'd often stub a toe,
And then I'd start a cryin' because it hurt me so.
Gramps would say, "Now stop that fuss.
The folks'll think you're dyin'.
Put on your happy face, come over here.
If you'll show your happy face, you're welcome here.
If you need a warm embrace, Step up, my dear.
To make a world, they say, it takes a bit of all kinds,
But show me your happy face any old time.
If you'll show your happy face, you can find friends.
If you have a warm embrace, joy never ends.
Some folks look for happiness but walk around blind
When they might be happy, if they'd only be kind."
Now, I've accepted Jesus; He is my friend.
With His love inside me, no need to pretend.
When I follow His way, His joy is mine,
And I can feel happy most of the time.

Truly Alone

In happy anticipation she used to wait there in her home
For the ding-dong of the doorbell or
the ringing of her phone.
Her heart was full and happy, for her life was full of fun,
Until the day they told her that the
love she knew was gone.
But still she went on waiting, till she got so depressed
That she could barely eat or sleep,
didn't feel like getting dressed.
Until police and ambulance came to the house next door.
Aimlessly she wandered out to see
what they were coming for.
Someone was wrapped up on a stretcher,
and she heard somebody say,
"Who'll look after her four children,
now that she has passed away?
She has no friends or relatives; her husband's in the San."
Oh Lord, she thought, *there's others*
much worse off than I am.
She's eating and sleeping better now, no time to feel alone.
There's an awful lot of work to do with
four children in her home.
Though she still needs adult company,
her heart sings a quiet song,
For her phone is often ringing and
her door bell goes ding-dong.

I Sing

I sing when I feel lonely; it drives my blues away.
I sing when I feel happy, so I'm singing every day.
I find when I am singing; it's easier to smile.
And when some joy I'm bringing,
living's more worthwhile.
When others think I'm happy, they feel happy, too,
For it isn't long when they hear a song
till a smile to come peeking through.
We should try not to stay unhappy,
For we spread a pall of gloom.
Others feel our sadness when we come into a room.
Find the right one to listen and tell what it's about,
You may find it isn't half as bad
When you've poured your story out.
If someone asks me why I'm happy, this is what I'll say:
"I feel that I am happy now. I poured some blues away.
And that is why I'm singing my happy little song.
I know now I am needed, and I feel that I belong."

Empty Heart

I can hear the children playing, smell perfume in the air.
Bits of joy and gladness are bubbling everywhere.
But I know a greater love, from all others set apart.
It fills the empty corners of a human heart.

Shades

Even the leaves danced to a rhyme
As we were walking there in the springtime.
The shadows played across her hair
As the sun went peeking here and there,
To see us sitting in the shade
In a quiet, long forgotten glade
Where birds and flowers seemed in tune.
The time was spring; the month was June.
Birds were chirping happily
When they flew to watch Mary and me.
Then a shadow passed o'erhead—
The scene was changed, Mary was dead,
And all the life and times between
Seemed to vanish like a dream.
Even the sun seemed not as warm
After Mary came to harm.
Though flowers bloomed,
They seemed not so gay,
And bird songs were something far away.
But now I've learned that life goes on,
With a deeper meaning, sadder song.
And just as the sun shines after rain,
Through pain and death, love blooms again.
Though not as bright as in days of yore,
The shades are deeper than before.

A Sunbeam

It splashes distant hill tops
With a crown of gleaming gold.
With all the breathless beauty
That a happy heart can hold.
Then it all blends in together
Into one majestic stream.
Then it flows along forever
With the smoothness of a dream.

I had a dream in which a special bell (or bells) guarded something precious, and would chime if some kind of harm seemed to be present or coming. Then it turned into one in which my younger brother had been playing music and had recorded it as a song to be sung at a wedding. It wasn't an ordinary song I'd heard before, though the first few lines are similar to my dream. I added a verse to it to capture more of the feeling.

Song of the Bells

The bells brought us a message so tender;
We'll always keep it in our hearts.
A love song of sweetest surrender
That told us we'd never part.
Our hearts will stay beating together
In the sweetest harmony ever sung.
No matter how rough be the weather,
Our life's song will always be one.
We'll have someone to love and to cherish
From the moment we each say, "I do."
Until the day that we perish,
To each other we will always be true.
Please, God, give us blessed guidance;
Thou alone know what is best,
So that when our love song is over,
We'll be clasped again to Thy breast.
Keep the bells of love softly ringing,
Echoing deep in our hearts,
So that they'll always be singing
The song they heard at the start.

How to Be Happy When Married

Kind consideration is all that it should take.
Romance just puts frosting on the cake.
But if I can't get my frosting, I'm apt to hit the roof.
It seems I was born with a sweet tooth.
Remember, he or she has feelings much like yours—
Don't fling them like garbage out the door.
For if you do, your future could be black;
We don't expect our garbage to come back.
At times I fear man of us are worth of the lash:
So many precious things are in our trash.

In My Valley

In my valley, my valley, I've found peace and rest.
Love beyond measure and real happiness.
The sound of children playing oft drifts on the air,
And a spirit of gladness exists everywhere.
There's warmth in people's faces
as I walk down the street;
Faces are friendly and open on the folks that I meet.
And the river so tranquil, winds lazily by
Until it blends in the distance with the blue of the sky.
If you want to reach my valley,
You must keep peace on your mind;
Don't fret or dally upon things left behind.
Always try to be cheerful as you go on your way,
And things that seemed fearful will soon fade away.
Think kindly of others, regard them as friends,
And you will discover a source of joy without end.
Don't repeat things about people unless they are good;
There are very few people who can do as they should.
When you do good to others and they do good to you,
A feeling of brotherhood can start to seep through.
You've found the trail to my valley, to real peace and rest;
You can know now how it feels to be truly blessed.

A Recipe for True Love

We'll never find true love if we don't know how to give.
If we don't know how to love, we don't know how to live.
If we think of other people and let them know we care,
We'll never get too lonely; someone always will be there.
When we love other people, we keep them in our heart,
So it never feels too empty whether near or far apart.
If we want nice other people, we use an age-old recipe:
We just be to other people the way we want them to be.

That's Why He Came!

Mankind is prone to sinning; it's in our very souls.
God knew from the beginning He
would have to make us whole.

(Chorus) That's why He came, that's
why He came. That's why
He came, came, came. That's why He came.

It took a lot of living to make me what I am.
It takes a lot of loving to save a mortal man.
(Chorus)

Now many know the story of how He left His realm above
To bring to us the glory of His great
redeeming love. (Chorus)

Now He's up in heaven, He sits at God's right hand
To assure for His believers entrance
to His Promised Land.
(Chorus)

Music

When the lovely music starts, joy
bells ring out in our hearts.
Then the happy teardrops start when
hearts are touched by music.
Let it ring out loud and clear, so we
can hear it far and near.
Music drives away our fears, and the
world seems bright with music.
Music is a common tongue, loved by almost everyone.
Music brings us so much fun. Say
"Hurray, hurray" for music.
Music eases cares away, add a cheerful note each day.
Lift your voices high and say, "Hurray, hurray" for music.
Music forms a heavenly strand that
links the heart of God to man
And helps to make us understand
life can be filled with music.
When we start to harmonize, joy tears well up in our eyes;
Then perhaps we realize hearts can be touched by music.
Music makes a happy sound to thrill
the countryside around.
The threads of love are closely wound
into our world of music.
Fish make sounds within the sea;
birds are singing in the trees.
God made each and all of these for us, His world of music.

The Spirit of Love

Soft and sweet as a new baby's breath,
The spirit of love ebbs and flows.
But until our eyes are closed in death,
It holds a secret that none of us knows.

We only know it's as precious and dear
As the blood that flows in our veins,
And all of the time we sojourn here,
It's the source of both joy and pain.

We know it can be given and returned,
But never taken back.
A truth that most of us will learn
Along life's rugged track.

But who can make love bloom again
In hearts that are weary and sad?
One who has known both sorrow and pain,
May have learned how to make some glad.

This person knows it's by being there,
Patient and undemanding;
Forgiveness on lips, a silent prayer,
A heart with understanding.

God's Invitation

All who are heavy laden, come, and I will give you rest!
Put your hand into My hand, and
your head upon My breast.
Know you not I feel the sorrow that
is spreading all abroad,
And that your life is truly precious
to the very heart of God?
Come for peace and understanding;
come, lose weariness of soul.
For My love makes you feel precious
with a body that is whole.
I love all of My creations; I see the sparrows fall.
But you are truly dearest, so I love you most of all.

Heart Song

Give me a love song that my heart can sing,
Like the warm gentle breezes that blow in the spring.
And if you will promise to always be true,
You can be sure that I'll always be faithful to you.
Like a sweet budding rose, you crept into my heart;
Now everyone knows what is likely to start.
When a love bud is growing, it is lovely to see,
And your eyes, softly glowing, look lovely to me.
Whenever I meet you, my heart starts to sing
Like a breath from the flowers that bloom in the spring.
My spirit bubbles over whenever you're near;
Like a bee in the clover, I'll buzz in your ear
And say all the nice things that I think you are.
Though other girls are pretty, you're nicest by far!

God's House

Oh! To sit in the house of our Lord,
To feel the touch of His hand,
To be uplifted by His word,
To have hope for His promised land.
God can fill the empty heart;
He can ease away our pain,
Put together broken parts,
And make it whole again.
We need only call on Him,
The saviour of our souls.,
He will wash away our sins
And make our broken spirits whole.
Oh! To be in love with our Lord,
To feel the exultation inside,
To be thrilled by His blessed word
And feel like a groom or bride.
To be healed by the blooming of faith
That bursts like the bud of a rose.
Through the knowledge of His saving grace,
May the buds keep bursting and grow.

A Single Parent Effort

With hope for joy to single parents everywhere,
We start off with a day of prayer,
To thank You, God, for all You've done and said;
For children, friends and daily bread,
For the forgiveness included in your plan
To lift the weight up off the heart of man,
That we may learn to lean on You each day
And know the peace and comfort in Your way.
During our week as we go through,
We'll try to share some of the things we do
To try to ease our loneliness
and try to have togetherness,
so that while living it's others we think of,
And learn that the joy in giving is true love.

God Is Light!

This is a simple factual statement, since He is
in and through all parts of His creation.
Light is the only portion of the electromagnetic
spectrum observable to us; without it,
the wonders of His creation could never
be revealed to the majority of us.
Each eye is a wonder of construction making
all the physical objects visible to us.
Not only is light necessary for our safety, but it reveals all
the beauties all around us and enables us to function in all
our walks of life. The physically blind have His inner light.
We say that Christ is the light of the world, which
is true when we realize He is God's son,
And without Him showing His love in all of His creation,
we would truly be in the dark literally, emotionally and
spiritually, unable to know the real joy that comes when
We feel completely whole, forgiven,
accepted and respected.

God is still the light when we haven't any sight;
He knows all our sorrows and fears.
Like the rose that crawled through a hole in
the wall, we will find He is always near.
May we all be like that rose, when we lie in sweet
repose, when we've reached the wall's other side.
Like the rose beyond the wall, in that land beyond
recall, may we ever grow in His grace.

May we be bathed in the light beyond the realm
of night, in the love shine of His face.
When we come to that day, it won't matter what
we say; there will be no air of despair.
We will go to our rest in the land of the blessed;
all His blessed believers are there.

(chorus) Like the Rose beyond the wall,
may we ever grow in His grace,
And unfold in perfection in the love-shine of His face.

I thank my God in heaven for the
thoughts He brings to me.
The wonder of His presence is like a haunting melody.
I can feel Him there inside me with every happy breath;
I know He wants to guide me till my
eyes are closed in death.
Then with this life over, I've gone beyond the mortal door.
The love and joy He showers on me,
will be mine forever more.

Rocket into Space

Man rockets outward into space, yet no
souls are saved without God's grace.
His children reach to touch a star and find
He is out there where they are,
In power for all to see.
Beyond the touch of human hands,
travelling through God's wonderland,
Eternity is but a step away.
The great will pray and humble be,
in awe of His great majesty,
For He still reigns.
Man hopes to reach the moon and soon step on the sand—
This date with fate, celestial real estate, ominous land.
No easy task, this hope to grasp a stairway to the stars,
To be the first in the universe, to
place a foot on moon or Mars.
Man, made of dust, eyed the lunar
crust; his hopes seemed vain,
Travelling in a mechanical monstrosity
to satisfy his curiosity
From whence he came.
Out there in prayer, His faithful find,
the secret of real peace of mind.
God is everywhere.

I pray the men from *Snoopy* and *Charlie
Brown* get back safely to the ground,
Having surveyed the grotesque scenery
like a witch's cauldron bubbling free,
Then froze in place pinnacles piercing a
cloudless sky with a black Earth riding high
In trackless space.
Having seen such raw creation, they'll
be the toast of man and nations;
They could glorify His holy name.
But if we could look at a new planet every hour,
through some of God's almighty power,
The programs that we would see could last for
countless centuries, for He still reigns.

May 1969

Time: The Great Healer

When our hearts are sore from weeping,
And our eyes have grown dim,
At a time we should be sleeping,
Do we ever think of Him?
With His trial of life near ended
And His battle nearly won,
He said, "Man, behold thy Mother;
Woman, behold thy son."
Or do we see the faded leaves
Aand observe the withered grass?
Like the dew drops of the morning,
The mourner's sorrow, too, will pass.

God's Presence

Do you feel He's close beside you,
That He counts your every breath?
Do you hope to be there with Him
In the life that's after death?
Do you think of each tomorrow
As a step closer to Him,
Or do you dwell upon your sorrow
Deep within?

(Chorus) If we look upon the bright side
As we go along life's way,
God will give us enough courage
for each day.

When you're feeling tired and weary,
And your eyes refuse to see,
Do you think of your Lord Jesus
And get down on bended knees?
This is where we find our comfort,
Though our hearts may feel they're torn,
For He gives a special blessing
To all of us who mourn.
(Chorus)

Do you feel you're all alone,
When you think about your loss?
Do you remember your Lord Jesus
As He hung upon our cross?
He said, "It is finished,"
As He drank the bitter cup.
Now our eyes are upon heaven,
And our hearts are lifted up.
(Chorus)

If we're feeling sad and lonely,
Cold and empty in our hearts,
We need to learn about our saviour
And the warm fullness He imparts.
Our hearts fill up with happiness
And not with blank despair,
And every breath we breathe
Becomes a thankful little prayer.
(Chorus)

A Parting Thought

My children are grown now, and off on their own.
I'm helping while waiting till He calls me home.
I wake up each morning with hope for each day;
I kneel down each evening and thankfully pray.
With my life in His service, my heart with His song,
The rest of my life won't seem very long.
But don't be too unhappy when I'm called away;
I've had many glad times with blessings each day.
Remember I'm happy, from all cares I'm free.
It's peaceful forever where I'm going to be.

Take Time for Love

Take time for love on the dismal days,
When the clouds above turn your sky to grey.
Make room for love and its tender times
When you're thinking of your valentine.

My Valentine

Do the words, "Will you be mine? I
want you to be my Valentine"
Still sound like music to your ears,
as they did for many years?
Although our hair does show some gray,
Our hearts can still feel young today.

If Only

If only I could capture the joyful, buoyant rapture
in her smile;
If I could discover the reasons why I loved her,
'Twould be worthwhile.
But who can grasp quicksilver, sunlight dancing on a river,
The twinkle in an eye?
The tinkle of her laughter, or the hug that followed after
A heavy sigh?
When I look up at night, at a myriad of lights
From distant spheres,
I don't think about her only, for you see, I've been so lonely
Through the years.
Do we really meet again, in a world beyond all pain,
Up in the sky?
Will she be waiting for me, and will she still adore me
As in days gone by?
I must leave it to God's will, for I know He's watching still
Our h0uman race,
And I'm sure that we will find,
somewhere in His good time,
We have our place.

Jesus

With His arms outstretched from His heavenly gates,
He gently entreats us and patiently waits.
Now here we are in our sorrows and fears,
Though His peace and joy has been calling
For over two thousand years.
Why do we reject Him? Why can't we obey?
We could accept Him—why not today?t out
one morning and looked up to the sky,
And felt overwhelmed by the beauty that met my eyes.
The sky was hung with lazy streamers
of such a dazzling white;
I thought that the angels must have
laundered them all night.
In between the streamers was a sky so wondrous blue;
I thought the angels must have washed the spaces, too.
After drinking in the freshness, I really must confess
None but our creator could make such loveliness.

Our House

Our house is one where kindness
dwells, we care for one another.
If someone needs help, somebody tells;
a kid, our Dad, or Mother.
We don't joke about important things;
it can get out of hand,
If someone feels hurt or angry, then,
we've spoiled our happy plan.
We try to keep our walk, our talk, always
clean and neat, we don't have to use the "street
talk" even when we're on the street.
So, if someone cold and empty, wants
a warm and friendly spot,
They'll find they're always wecome,
to share in what we've got.
The world is raucous, full of strife, but
there's something we've discovered,
There's so much more joy in life, when
we're kind to one another.

Christians, Arise!

Christians, arise! Shout Hallelujah up to the skies.
Pledge full allegiance, right to the end,
In a beautiful cadence to our Saviour and Friend.
His is the Glory we see here below,
His is The Story, to make our lives glow.
He has the mercy to ease us of pain,
He gives us His Grace to start over again.
Christ really loves us; He gave us His life,
No more can be given by husband or wife.
We can give our lives to each other,
through the example by Him,
Be true faithful lovers, and free from all sin.
The peace and contentment that He surely brings,
Removes all resentment and can make our hearts sing.
Life has new meaning; we're filled with His song,
On Jesus we're leaning, and feel we belong.
No more doubt or discourament, no envy or fear,
He gives us encouragement to find our love here.
For love is His reward, for a life that's well lived,
When filled with His love we find it easy to give.
We can love our neighbours, our family, and friends,
There's joy in our labour, and joy at the end.
We can fulfill His commandment to love one another,
And find contentment with our neibours as brothers.
For His Law is good, and brings peace to our souls,
When we do as we shold, we can feel that we're whole.
We're whole and forgiven, our past wiped away,
Our Hope is in Him, in His Heaven someday.
Live Him and Love Him to find peace of mind,

Put all your faith in Him, for He is so kind.
And yet He is powerful, a pillar of strength,
His Way is wonderful, He'll go to great lengths,
To saver us, His children made in the image of Him,
So we are able to be obedient, and not enslaved by sin.
When we ask Him for guidance, and simply obey,
Not yielding to questioning all of His Way.
He has the wisdom, our love is His,
Poured out there for us, that we might live.
Let opur hearts be thankful O God all our days.
Let our lives be fruitful, filled with Thy praise,
Let our voices be joyful, filled with Your songs.
Let our thoughts be beautiful, all the day long.
Hoping and working, thinking of Him,
From the time we are babies until our sight dims.
Until our steps falter, and He leads us Home,
Far across the still waters, no more to roam.
No more like lost sheep, who from
the Shepherd have strayed,
For now we are found, and the price has been paid.
Now we're considered worthy,
through the Blood of His Son,
To partake of His Glory, when our race is run.
He has the answers to the questions we have,
His is the Power through which we are saved,
He designed it all, in His heaven above,
His solution to our problems is through His infinite love.